MW01205528

JESUS IS LORD!

Exploring the Meaning of Jesus' Lordship

A BAPTIST DOCTRINE AND HERITAGE STUDY FOR LIFE TODAY

Howard K. Batson

BAPTISTWAYPRESS®

Dallas, Texas

Jesus Is Lord!

BAPTISTWAY PRESS® Management Team
Executive Director, Baptist General Convention of Texas: Charles Wade
Director, Missions, Evangelism, and Ministry Team: Wayne Shuffield
Ministry Team Leader: Phil Miller

Editor and publishing consultant: Ross West, Positive Difference Communications
Cover and Interior Design and Production: Desktop Miracles, Inc.
Printer: Data Reproductions Corporation

This book is produced in cooperation with the Baptist Distinctives Council/Texas Baptist Heritage Center of the Baptist General Convention of Texas—Executive Director Emeritus, BGCT, and volunteer Director, Texas Baptist Heritage Center, William M. Pinson, Jr.; Chair of Baptist Distinctives Council, Royce Measures.

First edition: November 2006
ISBN: 1-931060-85-1

*Dedicated to the faithful members of
First Baptist Church of Amarillo, Texas,
who have been proclaiming "Jesus is Lord"
since 1889.*

About This Doctrine, Heritage, and Life Study

This book—*Jesus Is Lord!*—is one of a series of books on Baptist doctrine and heritage that BAPTISTWAY PRESS® is producing annually.[1] These studies are intended both for individual reading and study and for group studies in churches and other settings.

The intent of this series is to provide guidance in considering, understanding, and acting on some of our deeply-held Baptist beliefs, particularly as these beliefs intersect with current life. The intent is *not* to produce an official statement about these Baptist beliefs. Even to attempt to do so would go against the very nature of who Baptists are.

So, as you read and study this book and the other studies in the series, be prepared to think seriously and carefully. Engage the ideas with your own thought and study, especially of the Bible.

In addition to this study book, suggestions for teaching this study are available in *Jesus Is Lord!—Teaching Guide*. See www.baptistwaypress. org for additional resources for this and other studies produced by BAPTISTWAY PRESS®.

The Writer: Howard K. Batson

Howard K. Batson is pastor of First Baptist Church, Amarillo, Texas. He is also the author of *Common-Sense Church Growth* as well as of numerous Bible studies for BAPTISTWAY PRESS®. He holds degrees from Lander University, Southwestern Baptist Theological Seminary, and Baylor University (Ph. D.).

Jesus Is Lord!

Introduction

THE EARLIEST FOLLOWERS OF CHRIST made the powerful declaration: "Jesus is Lord." This brief and seemingly simple affirmation of faith in Jesus is the most foundational and ancient confession of the early church. At the heart of all that the church believes is the Lordship of this Jewish rabbi who lived long ago. Only one idea—the Lordship of Jesus—serves as the foundation of Christianity, the anchor of the church. As we will soon discover in the chapters to follow in this book, the Lordship of Jesus serves as the very bedrock of the Christian faith.

A pastor in Atlanta, Georgia, with a tender heart for kids stopped at the Kool-Aid stand run by a couple of enterprising young girls in front of the home of one of them. He invested a quarter in their happiness. They handed him a cup filled with colored liquid.

As he sipped his sugary, watered-down drink, one of the little girls inquired, "Are you done yet?"

He still had some goo to gulp. So he replied, "No, why?"

The little girl set the record straight, "'Cause that's our only cup!"

The church, likewise, has only one "cup" from which all may drink, the cup of Christ's Lordship. There is no alternative for this foundation for Jesus' followers. To be a follower of Jesus is to call him *Lord*. When Saul (Paul) was persecuting the church, he was seeking to harm all who called on *the name* of the Lord (Acts 9:14, identified as "the Lord Jesus" in 9:17). When this persecutor of Christians became a persecuted Christian himself, Paul implored the Jewish crowd at the temple to "Get up and be baptized, and wash away your sins, *calling on His name*" (Acts 22:16, italics added for emphasis).[1]

So central is Jesus' Lordship to Christianity that Paul wrote with great confidence, "WHOEVER WILL CALL ON THE NAME OF THE LORD WILL BE SAVED" (Romans 10:13, quoting Joel 2:32, italics added for emphasis). When writing to the believers in Corinth, Paul described the church as "all who in every place *call on the name of our Lord Jesus Christ*, their Lord and ours" (1 Corinthians 1:2, italics added for emphasis).

The New Testament is clear that the Lordship of Jesus is the central belief on which all other Christian teachings are based. Therefore, we need to understand better what it means to say with our hearts and our heads that the man named Jesus is *Lord*.

What am I declaring when I call Jesus *Lord*? How do we understand Jesus' Lordship in light of the teachings of Scripture? Is my relationship to Jesus changed when I call Jesus *Lord*? If so, how? Is my relationship with others transformed when I submit to Jesus' Lordship? If so, how? Does calling Jesus *Lord* place any new demands on my life? If so, what? When I call Jesus *Lord*, how do I myself enter into the story of Jesus' Lordship? How will I deal with all of the other "gods" that demand equal or greater allegiance? Will my worldview be shaped by the fact that I follow Jesus?

If we understand the Lordship of Jesus, we will be able to grasp the central teaching of the early church and comprehend the very heart of the gospel. Because this book will bring you to the water from the deepest well of the Christian faith, your life might be transformed, your heart strangely kindled, and your mind refocused.

Be careful as you drink from the potent cup of Jesus' Lordship. Those who do are forever changed.

CHAPTER *One*

The Heart of the Christian Faith

To call Jesus Lord *is the heart of the Christian faith.*

THE FOREIGN EXCHANGE STUDENTS WERE eager to experience worship at a Christian church, to discover the essence of the Christian message. They had traveled from a culture that afforded them little exposure to the Christian faith. The group was visiting First Baptist Church of Amarillo, Texas, on two consecutive Sundays. It was their only opportunity to gain exposure to a Christian church while they were in the United States. They eagerly awaited the message from the interim pastor, Dr. Brad Creed, then Dean of George W. Truett Theological Seminary of Baylor University.

In his sermon, Dr. Creed told a story about a courageous lad named David who conquered an evil giant named Goliath. David conquered the giant, of course, using only smooth stones and a slingshot.

The next Sunday the students visited again, seeking to learn more about the Christian religion. This was the very Sunday I was to preach at First Baptist Church "in view of a call" to serve as pastor. In the midst of my preparation, I forgot to ask the obvious question, *Has anybody preached on 1 Samuel 17 lately?* I just assumed by choosing an Old Testament text I was safe from selecting a recently preached passage. I took the pulpit before the congregation and before the international students and began to preach as if my landing the job depended on it!

You guessed it! I was confidently expounding 1 Samuel 17, thinking I was leading the people through uncharted territory. I spoke of a courageous lad named David and his victory over the mean Philistine, Goliath! Everyone in the congregation wore the same pleasant grin, just as surely as the Dallas Cowboys wear matching helmets. Naively, I interpreted their expression as pride over the preaching of their soon-to-be pastor. I had no idea I had cluelessly and carelessly chosen to repeat last Sunday's sermon—a sermon impeccably delivered by the dean of the Baptist seminary!

The story line sounded familiar to the international students, too. They were hardly sitting on the edge of their seats pondering how the story ends. They were, unfortunately, all too familiar with the plot: the giant intimidates; the boy is courageous; the giant ridicules; the boy, with the help of God, conquers his fierce opponent. Knowing the end ruins even a good story.

Boy beats big man—to sum it up. The international students must have thought, *This is an interesting story, but who would ever build a religion around such a belief?* To them, the central hero of Christianity must have appeared to be a shepherd boy named David who was aided by a god to slay a giant. Perhaps they pondered, *What is the central meaning in this story? Could Christianity be teaching that good triumphs over evil despite the odds? Or that God will help you slay your giants?* They must have been perplexed, pondering why people would devote their lives to travel the globe and retell the story of the lad and the giant. Questions and uncertainty surely were swirling in their heads.

Of course, you know that David is not the central character of Christianity and that the climactic story line is not about the slaying of the Philistine champion Goliath. But all the international students had to go on was the two similar sermons, a repeated repertoire. Because they were misled by the double dose of David and Goliath, they still needed to find the heart of our faith.

Find Your Faith

Let's pretend. What if in their search for the core of Christianity the international students had chosen to interview you? Let's make the game even harder. If someone asked you to share your core beliefs in just three words, what words would you utter? Could you do it?

I am fully aware that I would have to give you pages, maybe even books, in which to write all that you hold to be true. But every great oak tree begins with a small acorn, and every river starts with a raindrop. From what seed does your faith grow? And from which droplet do your flood waters of faith flow?

As we read the letters and writings of the earliest Christians, we discover the source of what they held to be true about God, God's creation, and the relationship between God and his creation. Everything they believed, all that they held dear, could be summarized in the most profound statement ever articulated in human history: "Jesus is Lord!" All of Christian history, every word of Scripture, revolves around this central confession of the Lordship of Christ Jesus.

I am hardly claiming too much when I assert that "Jesus is Lord" was the prevailing confession of faith of early Christianity. New Testament scholar Robert H. Mounce declared that "Jesus is Lord" was Christianity's "earliest single-clause Christological confession."[1] Another New Testament scholar, George Ladd, called Jesus' Lordship "the heart of the early Christian confession."[2] Baptist scholar Stephen Hatfield stated that the Lordship of Jesus is found either implicitly or explicitly throughout Scripture.[3]

The central nature of this confession—"Jesus is Lord!"—is found prominently in the letters of the Apostle Paul. Salvation, for Paul, was defined by this central confession of Christ's Lordship. He wrote, "If you confess with your mouth *Jesus as Lord*, and believe in your heart that God raised Him from the dead, you will be saved" (Romans 10:9, italics added for emphasis). We find this key confession not only in Paul's letter to the church at Rome but also in his letter to the church in the city of Corinth. When Paul wrote, "No one can say, '*Jesus is Lord*,' except by the Holy Spirit" (1 Corinthians 12:3b, italics added for emphasis), he was affirming that "Jesus is Lord" is the most basic confession of

Christian fellowship. In Philippians, Paul envisioned a day when every member of the human race, both the living and the dead, would bow the knee to Jesus, a day when "every tongue will confess that *Jesus Christ is Lord*" (Philippians 2:11, italics added for emphasis).

Confessing the Lordship of Jesus distinguished members of the early church from the unbelieving world that surrounded them, for this confession encapsulated the heart of the faith and life of the Christian community. Therefore, unless we understand what it means to call Jesus *Lord*, we will never comprehend the essence of the message of the New Testament, the essence of all that was held to be true by the New Testament believers.

Before we can know what it means for us to call Jesus *Lord* today, we need to discover the ideas that were evoked when the word *Lord* (Greek, *kurios*) was used in the first century. Briefly examining the uses of the Greek word *kurios* in the ancient world in general, and in the Old and New Testaments in particular, will allow us to understand what early Christians meant when they called Jesus their *Lord* (*kurios*).

Uses in the Ancient World

Kurios, the Greek word for *lord*, was not invented by the early church but rather adapted by it. *Kurios* was such a common term by New Testament times that it appears in every New Testament book except Titus and the Letters of John. One of the most common uses of *kurios* in the ancient world was as a simple, polite form of address meaning *sir*. In a second century A.D. letter, Apion, a soldier in the Roman navy, wrote a letter to his father. His respectful form of address to his father was, "Sir" (*kurios*).[4] When *kurios* is used like this, as only an expression of courtesy, it does not carry any implication that the person being addressed is divine.

Biblical examples of this common usage of *kurios* are numerous. For example, before the Samaritan woman in John's Gospel knew the divine identity of Jesus, she addressed him politely as *kurios*, "Sir" (John 4:11, 15, 19). The Greeks who wanted an audience with

Jesus addressed one of the disciples, Philip, as *kurios* (John 12:20–21). The Apostle John recorded, "Now there were some Greeks among those who were going up to worship at the feast; these then came to Philip, who was from Bethsaida of Galilee, and began to ask him, saying, "Sir [*kurios*], we wish to see Jesus."

In addition to being used as a common, yet polite, form of address meaning *sir*, the Greek word *kurios* was also used as a term of royal distinction, often applied to rulers, governors, and caesars. In fact, on the Rosetta Stone, Ptolemy V, an ancient ruler of Egypt (about 205–181 B.C.), was identified as "Lord."[5] Further, in the first century A.D., although some Roman emperors rejected the application of the title to themselves, "the word slowly but surely established itself."[6]

A fine line exists between the use of *kurios* to designate a god and the use of that title to honor a ruler.[7] The Roman caesars gradually instituted a religion centered on themselves, a cult designed to increase their power. Christians believing in the exclusive Lordship of the risen Christ often refused to acknowledge an emperor as *kurios*. Despite the fact that Christians would give honor to the Roman emperor in other ways, their refusal to call Caesar *Lord* led to charges of insurrection and, oddly enough, atheism. Persecution or even execution by lions or fire sometimes awaited those devoted to the sole Lordship of Jesus.

One of the most notable stories of martyrdom surrounds Polycarp, Bishop of Smyrna around A.D. 155. Travel with me to the second century and witness his courageous faithfulness. Polycarp refused to acknowledge anyone other than Jesus as Lord. His story is powerful, and his devotion complete. Consider this paraphrase of what happened:[8]

> *They came after the old man, Polycarp, as if he were a common criminal, a dangerous outlaw. His friends had impressed on him the need to withdraw from the city to hide away on a small estate nearby. Passing time with the closest of friends, he prayed for fellow believers everywhere. He himself, however, had no heart for running, for he had placed his fate in the hands of God. Even the sheriff seemed a bit*

embarrassed that he was coming against such an old man as if he were in hot pursuit of a hardened criminal. When they finally found Polycarp in the hideaway estate, Polycarp left his upper bed chamber to come down to speak with his vigorous captors. The arresting officers were themselves puzzled that so much ado had been made over the arrest of a harmless old man. His crime was clear: because he believed Jesus was the only Lord, he had refused to acknowledge the lordship of Caesar.

Before they took him, the old man offered them food and drink and merely asked whether they would give him an hour to pray before he went with them voluntarily. Hearing his prayers, they even silently repented that they had come after so venerable an old man. The sheriff himself tried to persuade Polycarp: "Now what harm is there in saying, 'Lord Caesar' and in cursing the Christ to save yourself? Consider your age, old man. You are making too much of this." They were wanting Polycarp to deny his Christ by acknowledging the lordship of Caesar. "Go ahead. Call Caesar Lord!" the sheriff pleaded one last time.

But the old man silenced his captors, "I have served him for eighty-six years, and he has never done me wrong. How can I blaspheme my King who saved me?" With this stubborn refusal to identify anyone but Jesus as Lord, the mob shouted that he be fed to the lions. The official, however, chose instead to burn Polycarp alive at the stake. He gave his life in the flames of the fire to uphold the sole Lordship of Jesus!

Even before emperors were identified as *kurios*, the gods of the Orient and Egypt had long been called *lords.*[9] Because people were considered personally responsible to the gods who made them, the gods were thought to intervene in the lives of humans with rewards and punishments. For example, in one ancient Babylonian psalm (*Ungnad 220*), the writer pined, "As though I did not fear my god, my goddess, so it befalls me. Sorrow, sickness, destruction, and corruption are my portion."[10] Because of their perceived creative and controlling powers, the gods of the ancient world were deemed the lords of destiny and the lords of human beings.

Uses in the Old Testament

After the exile, Jews no longer permitted the pronunciation of the name Yahweh (the personal name for God).[11] Rather, they substituted *Adonai*, the Hebrew designation for *lord* or *sir*. In the Greek translation of the Hebrew Old Testament, the Septuagint, *Yahweh* was most often translated as "Lord" (*kurios*).

We can understand what it means to call Jesus *Lord* only when we comprehend that *Lord* is the name for God in the Old Testament. The Yahweh (in the Greek translation, *kurios*) of the Old Testament was much more than simply the Lord of the land or even of the people. With full prophetic power in mind, the Old Testament writers wanted to proclaim that their God, Yahweh, was Lord of all! For example, they called him "Lord of all the earth" (Joshua 3:11, 13; Micah 4:13; Zechariah 6:5; see also Psalm 97:5; Zech. 4:14).[12] The Old Testament God is called "Lord" because he holds power over the whole cosmos. He is both Creator and Sustainer of life. Thus, to say Yahweh is *Lord* is to summarize all of ancient Israel's beliefs, to summarize the whole Old Testament. The God who bears the name Yahweh is above all other gods.

The reader of the New Testament should be completely awestruck by the fact that so holy a designation, *kurios*, is applied to Jesus when the writers of the New Testament use Old Testament quotations about God (*kurios*) to describe Jesus. For example, when the fiery preacher, John the Baptist, stood and proclaimed, "Make ready the way of the Lord" (Matthew 3:3), he was applying to Jesus Isaiah 40:3, a passage about Yahweh. Too, in Matthew 4:7, we have a quotation from Deuteronomy 6:16, by which Jesus rebuked his tempter by telling him, "YOU SHALL NOT PUT THE LORD YOUR GOD TO THE TEST." At least secondarily, the passage makes Jesus "Lord . . . God," for Satan was being rebuked for tempting Jesus. Remember, Satan himself never really doubted the deity of Jesus.

To sum up, *kurios* was the translation of choice for the name of God, Yahweh, in the Greek Old Testament. Therefore, Old Testament passages that referred to God could be applied easily to Jesus by Greek-speaking Christians.[13]

Uses in the New Testament

God the Father is also called *kurios* in the New Testament. For example, Jesus said, "I praise Thee, O Father, Lord of heaven and earth ..." (Matt.11:25). In Revelation 4:11, moreover, the twenty-four elders fall down before God and worship him, saying, "Worthy are You, our Lord and our God, to receive glory and honor and power; for You created all things...."

So, in the New Testament, both God and Jesus are called *Lord*. Let's examine the types of literature found in the New Testament to find examples of *kurios* as applied to Jesus.

The Gospels

In the Gospels, Jesus often taught in the form of stories or parables. Many times, the central figure was a *kurios*, a lord. This lord was pictured as one in authority who came to pronounce judgment. For example, in Mark 13:33–37, the *kurios* (translated "master") of the house went on a journey and assigned certain tasks to his slaves. He appointed the doorkeeper to stay on the alert. Expecting the master's return at any moment, the subjects were to keep up their good work. The surprise return of the *kurios* ("master") in the story is representative of the return of Jesus the Lord at his *parousia* (Second Coming).

Jesus himself understood his ministry in terms of Lordship. In Mark 12:35–37, he quizzed the Pharisees concerning an interpretation of Psalm 110:1.[14] The question was clear: *If the Messiah was to be a descendant of David, how could David call his own son his Lord?* The implied conclusion asserted the deity of Jesus: The Lord (Messiah) was a descendant of David by physical birth, but David acknowledged the Lord (Messiah) as his spiritual authority. Because Jesus identified himself as the Messiah and because the psalmist addressed the Messiah as Lord, Jesus thus recognized the title "Lord" as applicable to himself.[15]

Of the synoptic Gospels (Matthew, Mark, and Luke), the Gospel of Luke gives special emphasis to Jesus as *ho kurios* (the Lord). New Testament scholar F.F. Bruce states that Luke referred to Jesus as "the

Lord" to remind his readers that the One about whom he was writing is now the risen and exalted Christ.[16]

In John's Gospel, moreover, Thomas addressed the resurrected Christ as "My Lord and my God" (John 20:28). With such a declaration, Thomas placed Jesus in a position equal to that of God.[17] The resurrection of Jesus led Thomas to make this exalted confession.[18]

The Book of Acts

The title "the Lord," which Luke used in his Gospel, is combined with other names by Luke in the Acts of the Apostles.[19] Jesus is called "the Lord Jesus" (Acts 1:21; 4:33), "the Lord Jesus Christ" (Acts 11:17), and "our Lord Jesus Christ" (Acts 15:26; 20:21).

In the Acts of the Apostles, the early believers were not using the word *kurios* to mean *sir* when applied to Jesus. Rather, *kurios* had developed into a confession of and commitment to the risen Christ.[20]

The early sermons in Acts are representative of the preaching of the early church. In these sermons, we have a gospel of Lordship. For example, in Acts 2:14–36, Peter, on the Day of Pentecost, stood before the crowd in Jerusalem and proclaimed his sermon. He related Old Testament texts concerning the Messiah to the life of Jesus. Peter then made the pivotal point when he declared, "Therefore let all the house of Israel know for certain that God has made Him both *Lord and Christ*—this Jesus whom you crucified" (Acts 2:36, italics added for emphasis). Using the same psalm that Jesus had employed to imply his Lordship, Peter made clear that Jesus not only had been crucified and resurrected but also is Lord of all (see Acts 2:34–35; Psalm 110:1).[21]

The Writings of Paul

Of all the biblical writers, Paul provides the most extensive instruction about the application of the title *Lord* to Jesus.[22] Out of the more than 700 times *kurios* occurs in the New Testament, more than a third are found in Paul's letters.[23]

In 1 Corinthians 12:3, Paul set forth the two basic mindsets of humanity. He declared, "No one speaking by the Spirit of God says

'Jesus is accursed'; and no one can say 'Jesus is Lord,' except by the Holy Spirit." Those who have the insight of the Spirit of God will declare the Lordship of Jesus.

In Romans 10:9, a passage we already have considered, Paul associated Jesus' Lordship with Jesus' glorious resurrection. For Paul, Jesus' Lordship was anchored in the resurrection act. Jesus' resurrection was both historically grounded and able to deliver humankind from the ultimate enemy—death.

In this same passage (Rom. 10:9–21), Paul asserted that Lordship breaks down ethnic barriers. He declared with boldness that there was no longer any "distinction between Jew and Greek; for the same Lord is Lord of all, abounding in riches for all who call upon him; for whoever will call upon the name of the Lord will be saved" (Rom. 10:12). Salvation itself, according to Paul, is found in the acknowledgment of the Lordship of Jesus, a salvation available to both Jews and Gentiles.

Other New Testament Writings

In other New Testament books, we find the same emphasis on Lordship. James declared, "My brethren, do not hold your faith in our glorious Lord Jesus Christ with an attitude of personal favoritism" (James 2:1).

Likewise, 1 and 2 Peter make the Lordship of Jesus apparent. Peter encouraged his readers who were living in the midst of suffering and persecution to "sanctify Christ as Lord in your hearts" (1 Peter 3:15).

Finally, Revelation portrays Jesus as Lord of the cosmos. He is ultimately declared as "KING OF KINGS, AND LORD OF LORDS" (Rev. 19:16). He is the slain and yet victorious Lamb who has taken on this wonderful name.

Early Baptists and the Lordship of Jesus

Baptist confessions of faith in the 1600s usually stated the Lordship of Christ in clear terms.[24] In the Somerset Baptist Confession of 1656, the Lordship of Jesus is described in terms of his offices: "our prophet; and king, lord, and law-giver"; "Prince of life"; "Prince of peace"; "Master of his people"; "Head of his church"; "the Almighty."[25] Another early Baptist confession declared in 1651 "that *Jesus Christ*, his Lordly or Kingly preeminence over all mankind, is vindicated or maintained in the Scriptures account by virtue of his dying or suffering for them."[26]

In seventeenth-century America, belief in the Lordship of Jesus bound scattered Baptist churches into a semblance of unity. Although the churches lacked general organization and had diverse backgrounds and leadership, they eventually formed a denominational organization because they recognized their common Lord.[27] Baptists throughout history have emphasized the Lordship of Jesus.

Placing emphasis on the Lordship of Jesus has shaped, at least partly, some foundational Baptist beliefs. For example, Baptists have believed in the autonomy of the local church (Baptist churches answer to no denominational authority) because each congregation is answerable only to the Lordship of Christ. Any other hierarchical arrangement would threaten the direct rule of Christ in his church. Also, emphasis on the Lordship of Christ led Baptists to realize the sole competency of the individual soul before God. Part of this conviction has been the idea that each person ought to be free to choose his or her own religion, apart from political compulsion.

Conclusion

We have seen that the early church moved quickly to centralize the confession "Jesus is Lord" as the heartbeat of its message. Whether we examine the letters of Paul to first-century churches, the historical record of Jesus' life as recorded in the Gospels, the preaching of the Apostle Peter as recorded in Acts, the brave stance of second-century Christians like Polycarp, or even early confessions of faith penned by Baptists in the seventeenth century, the core of Christianity emerges: "Jesus is Lord!"

Surely "Jesus is Lord" is the most powerful sentence that can be uttered by human lips. To say "Jesus is Lord" is to say it all!

But what do we really mean when we utter these words? How does it change our lives to make Jesus our Lord? The next chapters will help us consider and answer these questions.

CHAPTER *Two*

Jesus Is God

To call Jesus Lord
means Jesus is God.

How could Jesus be so different? He was from the little hamlet known as Nazareth, the son of a Jewish carpenter, a carpenter himself. Even the people of his own village took offense at his teaching, asking, "Is not this the carpenter, the son of Mary?" (Mark 6:3). How could this man—with hands nicked and scarred from the splinters of the woodshop—have the holy hands of God, hands that heal, hands that multiply a few loaves and a couple of fish until thousands are fed? Not only his neighbors, but even his own family, at one point, thought he had "lost His senses" (Mark 3:21; see John 10:20). Some were amazed that even the demons obeyed his voice; others were quite certain that Jesus himself was possessed by dark forces (Mark 1:27; 3:22).

This rabbi, teacher, chose the most unlikely people to be his students, and he went to parties thrown by sinners. His detractors labeled him "a drunkard" (Matthew 11:19), and his own disciples sometimes were shocked by his behavior. For example, in that culture men weren't allowed to speak to women in public places. Jesus, though, carried on a prolonged, personal conversation at the well with a questionable woman, a woman who lived with her boyfriend (John 4).

Despite all of his unpredictability, this rabbi declared a hopeful message about the rule and reign of God. People listened, for he taught with great authority (Matt. 7:29) and refused to be tamed by anyone. The crowds were hungry for hope, and so they listened and discovered God in an unlikely person, Jesus. They found God's voice in the voice of a carpenter.

The greatest questions ever posed by human lips were first asked by the first-century crowds who sat at this Jewish teacher's feet and by the scribes and Pharisees who tried to tame his tongue. They asked, *Is there some way in which this carpenter/rabbi is different from all the other teachers who talk about God? How can he be so human and yet speak as if God is his very Father? Is this man claiming to have the authority of God? Is he, in fact, divine? When we learn about him, are we also learning about God?*

Twins with Double Vision

This was a very big day for twin brothers in the third grade. They were coming to see me, their pastor, to talk about their pending baptism. The appointment was scheduled with great anticipation because each twin had made an individual commitment to Christ that was to be explored gently by me. The parents urged me to be careful, to make sure one twin wasn't simply following the other, because the boys did almost everything together. Promising the parents that I would not treat them as a pair but as individuals, I questioned each boy one-on-one.

In the midst of questions, I asked the first twin to share with me something that Jesus did during his lifetime, something that we might find him doing on any given day. The first twin replied with great confidence, "He would work in the woodshop with his dad." I didn't really remember a Bible story exactly like that from Jesus' childhood, but I did know that it was a logical and careful choice that demonstrated that the first twin saw the humanity of Jesus, his earthliness. He saw Jesus building a table in the shop with Joseph.

As I posed the identical question to the second twin during his sharing time, his answer was completely different. He immediately replied, "He preached about the Holy Spirit." While the first twin had seen the humanity of Jesus, the second son had seen the Jesus of the Trinity. He had seen the divinity of Jesus as expressed in his relationship to the Holy Spirit.

Which twin was right? They both were. Yet one had seen Jesus' humanness and the other had seen Jesus' divinity. Together, the twins had double vision—they saw Jesus as both human and divine.

Finding God by Finding Jesus

We can never understand the God of heaven unless we come to know him through his earthly Son. When renowned biblical scholar N. T. Wright was chaplain at Worcester College, Oxford, he had an opportunity to visit with freshmen for a few minutes on a one-on-one basis to welcome them to the college. Most of the students were cordial, but more than a few commented with a hint of confession, "You won't be seeing much of me; you see, I don't believe in God."

"Oh, that's interesting." Wright would reply, "Which god is it you don't believe in?"

The students were often taken by surprise because they regarded the word "God" as having only one meaning. Invariably, they would mutter a few defensive phrases describing the god they didn't believe in. Often, the god described was a caricature, a god who lived way up in the sky, looking down angrily at the world, randomly intervening with miracles, and sending bad people to hell while rewarding good people with heaven. Having patiently endured their distorted description of a whimsical old man, Wright would often reply, "Well, I'm not surprised you don't believe in that god. I don't believe in that god either."

The students were often startled by the chaplain's response until he continued, "I believe in the [G]od I see revealed in Jesus of Nazareth."[1]

As believers in Christ, we know about God because we know about Jesus. We understand God because we discover God in the person of his Son. To say "Jesus is Lord" is to say that Jesus is God.

Maintaining Monotheism

Jesus is one and the same with and yet not identical to the Lord, the Yahweh, of the Old Testament. Even though a first-century Jewish Christian would readily call both God the Father and God the Son *Lord*, there ultimately could be only one God in his or her belief system. Jews were monotheistic, meaning they believed only in the one God, Yahweh. At its root, Jewish monotheism asserted that there was but one God who was the Creator of heaven and earth. This God maintained an interest in and a dynamic relationship with his creation, especially humanity. Jews believed that God had called a special people, Israel (themselves), with whom to have a covenant relationship. God had rescued them from the bondage of Egyptian slavery. Jesus was so much God that early Jewish Christians could maintain their belief in Yahweh alone and yet also acknowledge Jesus as *Lord*. Calling Jesus *Lord* was in no way a denial of the oneness of God.

John, who was a Jewish follower of Christ, explained the relationship between the Father and the Son in the opening of the Gospel of John. He said that Jesus (the Word) was from the very beginning. He "was with God, and the Word was God" (John 1:1). Like God, Jesus was Creator. In fact, "all things came into being through Him" (John 1:3). If there was any doubt that John was referring to Jesus as "the Word," he made the connection clear, "The Word became flesh, and dwelt among us" (John 1:14).

Like John, Paul had no trouble being both a Jewish monotheist, believing in one God, and also calling Jesus *Lord*. In his first letter to the church at Corinth, Paul wrote, " . . . For us there is but one God, the Father, from whom are all things, and we exist for Him; and one Lord, Jesus Christ, by whom are all things, and we exist through Him" (1 Corinthians 8:6).[2] Paul was adapting the *Shema* (see Deuteronomy 6:4–5), a foundational Jewish affirmation that asserts God's oneness, to his belief that Jesus was equal with God.

Paul's Christ-centered monotheism is also found in Colossians 1:15-20. This passage declares Jesus to be the Creator of both the heavens and the earth. It declares that Jesus was "before all things" (Colossians 1:17), that he is "the image of the invisible God" (Col. 1:15).

Despite these definitive New Testament passages that unequivo-
cally declare Jesus as God, many readers of Scripture have concluded
that the New Testament writers never claimed divinity for Jesus. For
example, missing the mark, popular author Thomas Cahill concluded:

> . . . neither Mark nor Matthew, neither Paul nor Luke, none of the
> apostles and none of the disciples who gathered around Jesus and then
> formed the early church—considered Jesus to be God. This would have
> seemed blasphemy to them. Their belief in Christ was, after all, a form
> of Judaism; and Judaism was the world's only monotheism.[3]

Other scholars, moreover, are adamant that Jesus himself never
asserted his divinity. Theologian Marcus J. Borg, for example, stated
that we do not know whether Jesus considered himself to be the
Messiah or the Son of God and that Jesus did not teach this about
himself.[4] Borg thought that the church has claimed more for Jesus
than Jesus himself ever intended.[5]

Much of modern scholarship has concluded that Jesus was not
the Son of God. In fact, having surveyed a bundle of books, Philip
Yancey concluded,

> If you peruse the academic books available . . . you may encounter Jesus
> as a political revolutionary, as a magician who married Mary Mag-
> dalene, as a Galilean charismatic, a rabbi, a peasant Jewish Cynic, a
> Pharisee, an anti-Pharisee Essene, an eschatological prophet, a "hippy"
> . . . and as the hallucinogenic leader of a sacred mushroom cult.[6]

When we actually take a look at the Gospels, however, we have
clear indication that Jesus claimed to be divine, claimed to be God.
We see these claims in Jesus' words as well as his actions.

Ways the New Testament Writers Presented Jesus as Divine

Examining the New Testament reveals that there are many ways in
which it presents Jesus as divine. We see his divinity displayed by:

- His power to pardon
- His superiority over the Sabbath
- The truth in his trial
- Old Testament passages applied to the New Testament Christ
- Declarations from demons
- "Son of God" as a sign of sovereignty
- His keeping the gate to God
- Teaching that re-interprets the Torah, the Old Testament law
- John's portrait of a powerful Christ
- Tearing down the temple
- His worthiness to be worshiped

Let us consider each of these ways in which the New Testament presents Jesus as divine.

Power to Pardon

Jesus claimed to have the authority of God when he claimed to have the authority to forgive sins. Only the one wronged, God, has the authority to pardon a sin.

Jesus' claim to have the power to pardon sin was so repulsive that the religious authorities charged Jesus with nothing less than blasphemy.

I've imagined the dust and debris descending while Jesus was teaching in the scene portrayed in Mark 2:1–12. Suddenly, sunlight bursts through the roof. The crowd was so large that there was no other way to get their lame friend before the Lord. Persistence paid off as they slowly lowered his pallet through the roof until their friend rested right before the Teacher, before Jesus. When Jesus saw their great faith, he said to the paralytic, "My son, *your sins are forgiven*" (Mark 2:5, italics added for emphasis).

The scribes thought to themselves, "Why does this man speak that way? He is blaspheming; who can forgive sins but God alone?" (Mark 2:7). It was clear to the scribes that Jesus was claiming the authority of God when he asserted the authority to forgive sins. To have God's authority is to be God. Jesus was claiming to be divine.

Jesus, of course, could have corrected the scribes and made it clear that he was in no way presenting himself as God or as having God's authority. But instead, Jesus asserted his position even more strongly, "'But so that you may know that the Son of Man has authority on earth to forgive sins'—He said to the paralytic, 'I say to you, get up, pick up your pallet and go home'" (Mark 2:10).

Superiority over the Sabbath

As with exercising the power to pardon, Jesus demonstrated his divinity when he described himself as "Lord . . . of the Sabbath" (Mark 2:28). God himself had established the sacredness of the Sabbath. Therefore, only God could modify Sabbath observance. At the core of ancient Israel's commandments, we read, "For in six days the LORD made the heavens and the earth, the sea and all that is in them, and rested on the seventh day; therefore the LORD blessed the sabbath day and made it holy" (Exodus 20:11).

Picture Jesus' disciples out picking the heads of grain on the sacred day of rest, the Sabbath. The Pharisees loudly object because such harvesting amounted to work, at least according to them. Thus, the Sabbath regulations were being broken. Jesus wasted no time in asserting his authority, "The Sabbath was made for man, and not man for the Sabbath. So the Son of Man is Lord even of the Sabbath" (Mark 2:27b–28). Claiming to have the authority to redefine the status of the Sabbath was tantamount to claiming equality with God.[7]

Truth in the Trial

In Jesus' trial accounts, we find the clearest claim of divinity found in the Gospels. The charge against him was clear: "He made Himself out to be the Son of God" (John 19:7). Similar divine assertions are seen in Matthew's account. There the high priest said to him, "I adjure You by the living God, that You tell us whether You are the Christ, the Son of God" (Matt. 26:63). Jesus replied, "You have said it yourself; nevertheless I tell you, hereafter you shall see the Son of

Man sitting at the right hand of power, and coming on the clouds of heaven" (Matt. 26:64). This declaration of victorious power is a clear claim to deity.

During the trial events, Jesus made no attempt to redefine himself in acceptable terms. He let the divine claim stand. Again, the Jews found blasphemy in his divine description of himself (Matt. 26:65–66). To them, Jesus was worthy of death because Jesus had claimed what only God had the right to claim.

Old Testament Applied to a New Testament Christ

The Greek word *kurios* (Lord) was used in the New Testament to designate both God the Father[8] and Jesus.[9] This usage makes clear that Jesus was considered equal with God and was identified with God. For the Jew in particular, applying the term *kurios* to Jesus suggested that Jesus was equal with the Father.[10]

As stated in chapter one, the Greek Old Testament, the Septuagint, called the God of the Old Testament (Yahweh) *Lord* (Greek, *kurios*). *Lord* also denoted the name (Hebrew, *Adonai*) that was often substituted for *Yahweh* out of reverence for the divine name. Often New Testament passages referring to Jesus as *Lord* are quotations or applications of an Old Testament text containing one of the Hebrew names for God.[11] Applying the Old Testament word *Lord* to Jesus by using Old Testament passages to refer to him transferred the divine claims of God to Jesus.

For example, John employed Isaiah's foundational vision of the Lord (Isaiah 6:1–13) to imply that Isaiah was seeing the glory of Jesus.[12] According to John's interpretation (John 12:40–41), the Lord whom Isaiah saw on that occasion was Jesus. To see the glory of the Lord (Isa. 6:1) is to see the glory of Jesus: "These things Isaiah said because he saw His [Jesus'] glory, and he spoke of Him" (John 12:41). Moreover, in the Revelation, John declared Jesus as "Lord of lords and King of kings" (Rev. 17:14; see also 19:16). Here we find an echo from both Deuteronomy 10:17, "The Lord your God is . . . the Lord of lords," and Daniel 2:47, as Nebuchadnezzar acknowledged that Daniel's God was "God of gods and Lord of kings."

What could possibly allow the monotheistic Jews writing the New Testament to transfer to Jesus of Nazareth the Old Testament titles and activities that belonged to God alone? They believed that God himself had exalted Jesus so highly that God had declared the divinity of the Son. God had found his good pleasure in all those who "honor the Son even as they honor the Father" (John 5:23). In fact, if they refused to honor Jesus, they had refused to honor God. In refusing to give glory to the Son, one had not given glory to the Father. The Father has sent the Son.

Demons Declare It

Sometimes the disciples were doubtful in their decisions about the deity of Jesus. But the demons were decisive! Often, in the Gospel accounts, demons made a declaration of the divinity of Jesus just before they were cast out. For example, when the demon recognized Jesus as "the Holy One of God" (Mark 1:24), it was recognizing Jesus as being of God. This expression, "the Holy One of God," was not known as a messianic title or as a common Christian designation of Jesus.[13] Rather, the background of this phrase declared by the demons was the designation of God himself as the Holy One in the Old Testament.

For example, in Isaiah, we read, "'To whom then will you liken Me that I should be his equal,' says the Holy One" (Isa. 40:25). This passage is about the greatness of God. Or again, in Isaiah 57:15, we read, "For thus says the high and exalted One Who lives forever, whose name is Holy, 'I dwell on a high and holy place. . . .'" Therefore, the demons themselves recognized the divinity of Jesus.

On another occasion, Jesus left the boat, and, almost before Jesus' feet touched dry land, a demon-possessed man who hid among the tombs ran to meet him—a man so powerful that he could not be contained by chains. The demons dwelling within the man cried out with a loud voice, "What business do we have with each other, Jesus, Son of the Most High God? I implore You by God, do not torment me!" (Mark 5:7).[14]

The demons perhaps had learned well from the chief of the underworld, Satan. Remember the temptation story? Satan did not challenge Jesus with the words "If You are the *Messiah*," but "If You are the *Son of God*" (Matt. 4:3, italics added for emphasis) indicating that Satan himself was aware of Jesus' divine claim. Demonic recognition of Jesus' deity was immediate and direct.[15] The demons often approached Jesus making supernatural, instinctive declarations of Jesus' divinity. As Mark summarized, "He was not permitting the demons to speak, because *they knew who He was*" (Mark 1:34, italics added for emphasis). In contrast, the demon-possessed girl in Acts 16 called Paul and his missionary company "bond-servants of the Most High God" (Acts 16:17). The demons even knew the difference between the divinity of Jesus and the humanity of the apostles.

"Son of God" as a Sign of Sovereignty

The title "Son of God" is used in the Gospels to indicate Jesus' divinity. This title is applied to Jesus in the opening words of the Gospel of Mark: "The beginning of the gospel of Jesus Christ, the *Son of God*" (Mark 1:1, italics added for emphasis). Likewise, as Jesus posed the question "Who do you say that I am?" Peter confessed, "Thou art the Christ, the *Son of the living God*" (Matt. 16:16, italics added for emphasis).

At momentous occasions in the ministry of Jesus, Jesus was repeatedly declared as the Son of God: at his baptism (Mark 1:11); at the temptation experience (Matt. 4:3, 6); at his transfiguration (Mark 9:7); and at his trial (Matt. 26:63). Even as Jesus was dying on the cross, his divine claims were mockingly thrown back into his face: "If You are the *Son of God*, come down from the cross" (Matt. 27:40, italics added for emphasis). At the climax of the drama on the cross, the temple veil was torn asunder, earthquakes rattled the land, boulders burst, and saints escaped their tombs (Matt. 27:51–52). Amidst all the cosmic commotion, a centurion who was keeping guard at the foot of the cross shouted with great fear, "Truly this was the *Son of God!*" (Matt. 27:54, italics added for emphasis).

Not surprisingly, the letters of the New Testament also employ the divine title, "Son of God," as a favorite designation for Jesus. He is called the Son of God four times in Paul's letters,[16] four times in Hebrews,[17] and eight times in the Letters of John and the Revelation.[18]

Gatekeeper to God

So closely related are the Father and the Son that Matthew described their relationship in a unique way. Matthew did so in what has been called the most important passage in the synoptic Gospels when studying Christ (Matt.11:25–27).[19] Here Jesus claims that while God has hidden his divine revelation from the wise of this world, all things have been handed over to the Son by the Father. Jesus continued, ". . . and no one knows the Son except the Father; nor does anyone know the Father except the Son, and anyone to whom the Son wills to reveal Him" (Matt. 11:27).[20] Jesus' knowledge of the Father is direct and immediate. Humanity may enter into the knowledge of God only through revelation by the Son. Therefore, as the Father exercises power in revealing the Son, the Son exercises complete control in revealing the Father to whom he chooses.

Teaching That Re-interprets the Torah

Jesus' teaching was unique; he didn't teach like the other rabbis. As Mark concluded, "They were amazed at His teaching; for He was teaching them as one having authority, and not as the scribes" (Mark 1:22). In Jesus' most noted sermon, the Sermon on the Mount, he taught as if he himself had something to say that was on par with the writings of Moses and the law of God (the Torah). He repeatedly used the formula, "You have heard . . . but I say. . . ."[21] For example, Jesus declared, "You have heard that it was said, 'YOU SHALL NOT COMMIT ADULTERY'; *but I say to you*, that everyone who looks on a woman with lust for her has already committed adultery with her in his heart" (Matt. 5:27, italics added for emphasis). Or again, "You have heard that it was said, 'YOU SHALL LOVE YOUR NEIGHBOR and hate your enemy.' But I say to you, love your enemies and pray for those who persecute you. . . " (Matt. 5:43–44).

Jacob Neusner, a premier scholar on Judaism of the Christian era, pondered the question of how he would have responded to these powerful teachings of Jesus. Neusner believed he would have been impressed with the Sermon on the Mount as he sat in the crowd, soaking up the wisdom from this rabbi of Nazareth. At the same time, however, Neusner concluded that he would, finally, part company with Jesus because Jesus began to move the emphasis from the Jewish community to himself. He had begun to shift from the law, the Torah, to himself as the central authority. Neusner concluded that Jesus was making a demand that only God could make. Although Neusner said *no* to Jesus, at least he recognized that Jesus called for the devotion that one would give only to God.[22]

Tearing Down the Temple

The temple in Jerusalem was the symbolic heart of Judaism. This sacred place represented the very home of Yahweh, the place where forgiveness from God was accomplished through sacrifice. Thus, the temple represented fellowship with God.[23] Jesus, though, attacked the status quo of the temple system by turning over the tables of the moneychangers (Matt. 21:12) and by speaking of the temple itself being torn down (Matt. 24:1–2; 26:61; see also 27:40; Mark 14:58; 15:29; John 2:19–20). In doing and saying these things, Jesus was asserting that God was going to dwell among his people, a new people that would include both Jews and Gentiles, in a way that could not be contained by bricks and mortar. New Testament interpreter N.T. Wright suggested that Jesus acted as if his own movement was a God-given replacement for the temple.[24]

By his statements about the temple, Jesus showed that he was claiming to have the very authority of God. When Jesus arrived at Jerusalem, in a sense the city wasn't big enough for both Jesus and the temple. Jesus took the temple, especially in its corrupt form, head on. As Jesus turned over the tables, he was embodying an acted parable, the symbol of judgment—like physically tearing up a contract to show it no longer is valid.[25]

In essence, Jesus was saying that the temple no longer deserved to be considered God's house but that it was time for it to be torn down.[26] At his trial, the words Jesus uttered about the temple were both remembered and resented by the Jewish leaders (Matt. 26:61). His accusations against the temple system represented no small portion of the desire to crucify him.

As Jesus celebrated the Passover meal with his disciples a few days after he had disrupted the temple by turning over the tables, he turned the symbolism of the meal in a new direction (Matt. 26:20–30). The real Passover lamb was about to be sacrificed, and real liberation was about to be enacted. For Jesus, the new kingdom of God would not be found in rebuilding the temple with bricks and mortar or in leading a military revolution against the Romans. It was going to come with his crucifixion and resurrection. Too, the new temple—representing God's saving presence—was found in Jesus himself. The temple had been the central "incarnational" symbol of Judaism, representing the place where heaven and earth interlocked, the place where God was present with his people. Now God was present in the person of Jesus. The temple was no longer needed.[27]

Jesus embodied the glory of God, tabernacling with his people. Jesus was claiming to be the place where Israel's God was at last personally present with his people.[28] Jesus could replace the temple, for Jesus was the presence of God (*shekinah*) once found in the temple. As John said, "The Word became flesh and tabernacled in our midst" (John 1:14, author's translation).[29]

Jesus was, at the heart of his teaching, remaking the people of God around himself! He claimed to be able to offer people the type of blessing they could get only from God himself.

John's Portrait of a Powerful Christ

If the reader of the synoptic Gospels (Matthew, Mark, and Luke) had any doubt about Jesus' claim to be divine, when we explore the Gospel of John the picture is all the more clear.[30] In John 10:30, Jesus even claimed to be one with the Father. This claim evoked rage from the Jews who "picked up stones again to stone Him" (John 10:31). The Jews fully realized that Jesus was placing himself on par with God. When Jesus asked them why they were about to stone him, they replied, "for a good work we do not stone You, but for blasphemy; and because You, being a man, make Yourself out to be God" (John 10:33). The Jews of John's Gospel interpreted Jesus' statements as divine claims.

On another occasion, Jesus claimed that to see and know him was to see and know the Father (John 14:7–9). When Jesus' disciple Philip requested to see the Father, Jesus rebuffed him. He assured Philip that he had no need to see the Father because, "He who has seen Me has seen the Father; how can you say, 'Show us the Father'?" (John 14:9). Jesus made it clear that he is in the Father and the Father is in him (John 14:10).

In John's Gospel, Jesus also claimed to be the *I Am*, a name that reminds us of the Lord (Yahweh) of the Exodus ("I am," Exodus 3:14–15). As God identified himself as the *God of being*, so did Jesus!

In John 8:58, Jesus even claimed preexistence, "Truly, truly, I say to you, before Abraham was born, I am." Claiming to be the Messiah, Jesus said, "I who speak to you am He" to the woman at the well (John 4:26).[31]

In John's Gospel, Jesus also claimed to be simultaneously working with God when he declared, "If anyone loves Me, he will keep My word; and My Father will love him, and We will come to him and make Our abode with him" (John 14:23). This language made it clear that when God was at work, Jesus was at work with him.

The Jews understood the words of Jesus found in John's Gospel as blasphemous, as a direct claim of divinity. Their response was predictable; they picked up stones to cast at him (John 8:59). As the law makes clear (Leviticus 24:16), stoning was the prescribed penalty for blasphemy, for claiming for oneself what belonged only to God.

Jesus' Worthiness to Be Worshiped

The early Christians, said New Testament scholar N.T. Wright, came quickly to believe they should worship Jesus even though they were Jews who believed in only one God.[32] Paul spoke of Jesus not only in the same breath that Paul spoke of the one God, but actually within such statements (see 1 Cor. 8: 6; Gal. 4:1–7; Phil. 2:5–11; and Col. 1:15–20).

The New Testament writers presented Jesus as being worthy of the worship offered to God himself. For example, Jesus healed a man who had been blind from birth. While the man immediately regained his vision, he only gradually saw Jesus as someone worthy of the worship he had previously directed to God alone. At first, he called his healer "The man who is called Jesus" (John 9:11). Next, he called Jesus "a prophet" (John 9:17). Finally, he saw not only physically, but also spiritually. He then said, "Lord, I believe," and worshiped Jesus (John 9:38).

Conclusion: Riots in the Street

Whether he claimed to have the power to pardon sins or declared himself to be Lord of the Sabbath, Jesus clearly presented himself as being one with God. We can never overestimate the importance of Jesus' deity. Whenever people have been uncertain about the closeness of Jesus to the Father, they have also lost the certainty of their Christian hope.[33]

What we believe about Jesus really does matter. While we should all choose our clashes carefully, the divinity of Jesus is worth the struggle. If we really understood that unless Jesus is God he cannot save us, then we might affirm more vigorously Jesus' divinity.

Could you imagine riots in the streets today over the issue of the divinity of Jesus? In the third and fourth centuries of the church, there was a charismatic and persuasive young church leader in Alexandria whose name was Arius (about A.D. 250–325). He led a mini-rebellion against the Bishop of Alexandria, whose name, confusingly enough, was Alexander. Alexander had preached a sermon that, for Arius, came too close to saying that Jesus was completely God. Arius was certain that Alexander had placed Jesus in a relationship so close to God that he was completely denying the humanity of Jesus, making him only divine.

As a result, Arius started a campaign—with sermons and pamphlets—teaching that Jesus was *not* equal to the Father, but was a creature—a created being. The Bishop of Alexandria, Alexander, called a meeting of bishops to examine the ideas of Arius and rule on whether they were acceptable. Knowing he was under examination, Arius and his followers marched through the streets of the city and around the bishop's house with signs that said things like, "There was a time when the Son was not." They made up sing-along songs to the same effect. In fact, there were eventually some street clashes over the issue of the humanity versus the divinity of Jesus. When the group of bishops met, they understood that if Arius was allowed to strip Jesus of his divinity, then the terrible thing would be true: if Jesus was not God, he could not reunite us with God.

The conflict continued, escalating until the Emperor Constantine called for the bishops of the Empire to come to Nicea and reach a compromise that would bring unity to the church. Therefore, in A.D. 325, more than three hundred bishops met together and concluded that Jesus was indeed God. The speech defending Arius began with the fatal error of denying that the Son of God was divine. Arius declared Jesus to be a creature who was not equal with the Father in any sense.

Some of the bishops in the room actually covered their ears and shouted as they tried to drown out his heresy. Others snatched the document out of his hands and stomped on it. What came to be known as the Nicean (or Nicene) Creed was adopted. The Nicean Creed declares that there is one God, and one Lord Jesus Christ, the Son of God, who was true God of true God, of one essence with the Father, by whom all things were made.[34]

Down through the decades, Christians have followed in Alexander's footsteps, refusing to allow anyone to cast aside Jesus' claim to be divine, to be the embodiment of God himself. For example, C. S. Lewis observed that there is little room for middle ground when it comes to the person of Jesus. Lewis concluded that it is foolish to label Jesus simply as some sort of great moral teacher while rejecting his claim to be God. Lewis asserted, "Either this man was, and is, the Son of God: or else a madman or something worse. You can shut Him up for a fool, you can spit at Him and kill Him as a demon; or you can fall at his feet and call Him Lord and God."[35]

Everyone must eventually answer the most important question ever articulated: *Who was Jesus?* What will you decide about Jesus? Was Jesus God?

CHAPTER *Three*

The Kingdom Has Come

To call Jesus Lord *means the kingdom of God has come.*

THE DOCTOR HAS TAKEN CERTAIN tests and sent them away to be read. Because of the holiday weekend and the backlog of patients, you won't likely hear any results for two weeks. The clock creeps along at a snail's pace. During the torturous waiting period, you imagine the worst, hope for the best, and figure out how to settle for something in between. You replay the doctor's visit a thousand times in the middle of the night. You try to read the doctor's face and expressions—a raised eyebrow, a cluck of the tongue, the tone of voice. Then your mind shifts to the technician and the technician's guttural groans and nervous fingers. Do any of these hold the answer? Or do they mean nothing at all? How can you tell the difference?

You're a six-year-old girl and can't wait until Christmas. Your parents have promised, or at least hinted, that Santa Claus is going to bring you a Welsh pony. You've already been riding a friend's pony since you were four years old, but you dream every night of having a pony of your own. You are picking out possible names: Scout, Teddy Bear, Charm, or Thunder. In your grandest dream, the pony is a gray gelding, but any color will do. *How long 'til Christmas?* you ask your mother. She responds with a sly grin that indicates she might have just been shopping for a pony. *Thirty days*, comes her tempting reply. Every hour becomes a day. Every day becomes a week. Every week becomes a month. And the month seems a year. How can Santa be so slow and Christmas approach at such a crawl? You are forced to wait and to ride your Welsh pony only in the meadows of your mind. Time has never stood still as it does for the child waiting for a Christmas surprise.

You've been sleeping on a slab of cold concrete for forty-one months. Every day is the same monotonous routine: eagerly awaiting your ration of one bowl of sticky rice and waiting at the well for hours to fill your canteen with water. The balance of each day is spent longing for liberation. As a prisoner of war, you have been beaten badly on the Bataan Death March. You're lucky enough to be counted among the 54,000 who survived the sixty-mile-plus trek from the Bataan Peninsula to a P.O.W. camp in the north and not among the thousands who died along the way. Every day you languish with fellow prisoners, hoping that help is on the way. You try not to cross the enemy guards for fear of a bayonet being thrust between your shoulder blades when you turn your back. The only thing that keeps you alive is hope for home and warm memories of family and friends. The letters you send are never really mailed, and those you are supposed to receive are never delivered. The silence is deafening, and the wait causes worry. You have no idea when the end will come or even if the end will come. You can only wait. Forty-one months and counting. Three and a half years on a concrete cot like a caged animal. Will you ever be released? Will you ever be home again?

Sometimes the waiting time is the hardest time of all. It is the time in between where we are now and where we hope to be. Whether two weeks or two decades, waiting time is torturous time. That was so in biblical times, too.

Looking and Longing—An Old Testament Perspective

The Day of the Lord

The ancient Israelites had been waiting for the great "day of the Lord" when God would intervene on their behalf, overturning injustice, righting all wrongs, and freeing them from the oppression of foreign rule.[1] The day of the Lord was an event more than a date. It was usually represented as God's intervening on behalf of ancient Israel and judging the pagan nations. This event would put an end to human rebellion and begin the period of God's complete sovereignty (Joel 2; Isaiah 13–14). The day of the Lord was the hinge point that connected human history with the eternal kingdom of God. Sometimes the Old Testament referred to it as "those days" (Jeremiah 5:18; Joel 3:1) or the "time" that was coming (Joel 3:1). Although described in various terms, the event was the same—the arrival of God's reign in human history.

Of all the elements the day of the Lord might have included from an Old Testament perspective, we can be sure that the occasion held at least three hopes of God's people: (1) God acting in the here and now; (2) judgment on those who opposed Yahweh; and (3) the liberation of ancient Israel from all pagan authorities. The description of the day was one of wrath, anguish, affliction, destruction, and devastation, which reached its climax in the picture portrayed in Zephaniah: "a day of trumpet and battle cry against the fortified cities and the high corner towers" (Zeph. 1:16).[2] According to the prophets, all of history was moving toward this great climactic moment when God would intervene on behalf of God's people.

The day was also, however, to be a day for the purification of the people of God. The prophetic word declared, "Behold, I am going to send My messenger, and he will clear the way before Me. And the Lord, whom you seek, will suddenly come to His temple" (Malachi 3:1). The question is then asked, "But who can endure the day of His coming? And who can stand when He appears?" (Mal. 3:2). No answer is given, but it is said that the Lord himself will bring about the purification of his people "like refiner's fire and like fullers' soap" (Mal. 3:2). The day of the Lord, therefore, represents God's arrival and the arrival of God's kingdom as God purifies his people.[3]

The Kingdom of God

The ultimate purpose of the day of the Lord is that the kingdom of God might be established. While the expression *kingdom of God* is never actually used in the Old Testament, God is called "King" forty-one times in the Old Testament.[4] For example, Psalm 29:10 states, "the Lord sits as King forever," and Isaiah was fearful for his life because his "eyes have seen the King, the Lord of hosts" (Isa. 6:5).[5] God is so clearly and consistently pictured as King that one of the foundational elements of faith in the Old Testament is that God is the ruling Lord. God's kingship is related to God's sovereign acts on behalf of his people through all the ages. Zechariah, the prophet, looked forward to the day when "the Lord will be king over all the earth; in that day the Lord will be the only one, and His name the only one" (Zech. 14:9).[6]

From the Old Testament, we glean several truths about the kingdom of God. First of all, it provides *the universal rule of Yahweh*. This realm of God's rule includes both Israel[7] and the Gentiles who turn to God so that God's kingdom knows no boundary in regard to the nations. All people will submit to God.[8] The nations are included also in the salvation of that kingdom.[9] While God is already King in one sense, God must one day fully manifest his kingship in the world of people and nations.

The second element of God's kingdom is *righteousness*. The kingdom of God provides a time of cleansing, renewal, and justice.[10] Sometimes the righteousness of the Messiah himself overflows to the people (Isa.11:3–5; Jer. 23:5–6), and sometimes the righteousness is found among God's people in general (Isa. 26:2; 28:5–6). The arrival of the kingdom ushers in a new kind of righteousness as the Lord seeks the cleansing and renewal of his people.

A third element of the kingdom of God is *peace*. War ceases among the nations (Isa. 2:2–3; 9:5–6; Micah 5:4–5; Zech. 9:9–10), and there is even peace among the animals (Isa. 11:6–7; 35:9). Paradise-like life returns with expectations of overflowing fruitfulness in nature.[11] God is at peace with humanity, and people are at peace with one another. This peace represents salvation.[12] Therefore, all of human history is striving toward the goal of the coming of the kingdom of God, which includes God's complete sovereignty, righteousness, and peaceful salvation.

Looking and Longing—A New Testament Perspective

The Kingdom of God

Even though the phrase *the kingdom of God* is never actually used in the Old Testament, by the first century both the arrival of God's reign and God's continuing rule on earth had been encapsulated with those words. All that God's people hoped for, in fact, had been wrapped up in the terms *kingdom of God* or *kingdom of heaven*.[13] The kingdom represented a time when all God wanted to accomplish would happen on earth as it already did in heaven, even as our Lord's prayer longed for such a day (Matthew 6:10).

But the real questions for first-century Jews were how, when, and through whom was God's kingdom going to arrive.[14] Israel had waited for God's restoring hand since the fall of Jerusalem in 587 B.C., when their Babylonian conquerors had carried them as captives into exile. Although long since released from captivity, the ancient Israelites had never fully enjoyed freedom. God would eventually reign, for ancient Israel had depicted God as King of both Israel (Exod.15:18; Isa. 43:15) and all people (Jer. 3:17; Zech. 14:9). His sovereign rule would, at last, bring forth their long-awaited liberation from foreign powers.

While You Are Waiting

By the first century, various approaches had been developed to try to deal with the delayed coming of God's kingdom. One approach was taken by the Qumran community. This community, which produced the Dead Sea Scrolls, simply withdrew from the wicked world and waited for God to do whatever God was going to do. They chose isolation.

Others, like Herod, built palaces for themselves and tried to get along with the ruling power of that day—Rome—in hope that God would some day validate their feeble compromises with worldly powers. They chose to enjoy the earthly rule of Rome while at the same time many of them also waited for the kingdom to come.

The Zealots took the most aggressive approach, however. They were ready to take political action. They sharpened their swords to fight a holy war to put God on the throne even as they said their prayers.[15] They chose to try to force the kingdom's arrival by initiating a kingdom clash between worldly powers.

Jesus and the Presence of the Kingdom

The question, of course, is, *What was Jesus' approach? How did Jesus look and long for the kingdom of God?* Surprising his contemporaries, Jesus proclaimed that the kingdom of God had already arrived with his very presence. The summary of Jesus' preaching, as presented by the Gospel writers, is certain and succinct: "Repent, for the kingdom of heaven *is at hand*" (Matt. 4:17, italics added for emphasis). The center of Jesus' message was the kingdom of God.[16] Jesus was declaring that God was, indeed, implementing God's age-old plan. God was pressing his sovereignty on Israel and the world and promoting justice and mercy.

God was accomplishing all this through Jesus himself. As Lord, Jesus was teaching and acting as if the very plan of God's salvation and God's vindication of Israel was actually occurring because of Jesus' own presence and work. Many of Jesus' parables concerned the arrival and the value of God's kingdom (Matt. 13; Mark 3:27; Luke 15). Jesus was declaring that those who heard his message should give up their approaches to bringing in the kingdom or dealing with its delay. Rather, they should devote themselves to Jesus' new vision of God's reign and rule.

Jesus' most famous sermon, the Sermon on the Mount (Matt. 5–7), is a seedbed for Jesus' teaching about the kingdom. Jesus told his disciples, "Do not resist an evil person; but whoever slaps you on your right cheek, turn the other to him also" (Matt. 5:39). With these words, Jesus was declaring that his followers should not join the Zealots in their approach to inaugurating the kingdom. Rather, Jesus' hearers were to fulfill the role of God's people, the role of Israel—to be the light of the world, the salt of the earth, and a city set on a hill that cannot be hidden (Jerusalem; see Matt. 5:14–16).[17]

The kingdom Jesus proclaimed had its roots in ancient Israel, but it grew in a new direction. Jesus was declaring that he and his followers were now the true people of God, the reconstituted Israel. They too would experience suffering, but God would ultimately vindicate them.

Whether Jesus was commanding directly, "Repent, for the kingdom of God is at hand" (Matt. 4:17), or teaching from the prophets in the synagogue, his message was the same: *That which the prophets have spoken of has begun in me* (see Luke 4:21). In Luke 4 we have the central passage of the Gospel of Luke. Jesus took the scroll of Isaiah, stood in the synagogue, and read: "The Spirit of the Lord is upon Me, because He anointed Me to preach the gospel to the poor. He has sent Me to proclaim release to the captives, and recovery of sight to the blind, to set free those who are oppressed, to proclaim the favorable year of the Lord" (Luke 4:18; see Isa. 61:1). Next, Jesus, as was customary, rerolled the scroll and sat down to expound on the prophetic passage. With all eyes fixed on him, Jesus made the great declaration that the kingdom of God had arrived, saying, "Today this Scripture has been fulfilled in your hearing" (Luke 4:21).

In the kingdom of God, the downtrodden, infirm, and marginalized poor were to be uplifted by God's righteous hand. Jesus was accomplishing the very tasks that were identified with the agenda of God's kingdom.

When John the Baptist was held captive by Herod, John sent his disciples to ask Jesus whether Jesus was the "Expected One" or whether they should look for another (Luke 4:19). Jesus gave evidence of his position by declaring that his answer was found in his actions, "Go and report to John what you have seen and heard: the blind receive sight, the lame walk, the lepers are cleansed, and the deaf hear, the dead are raised up, the poor have the gospel preached to them" (Luke 7:22).

The crowd who heard Jesus preach in Luke 4 was so shocked that the son of Joseph, a carpenter's boy, claimed to have inaugurated the new age and thus to have brought in the year of the Lord, that they were filled with rage (Luke 4:28). They were ready to kill Jesus. Only by God's miraculous hand was Jesus able to escape from his hostile countrymen (Luke 4:30).

With the declaration that Isaiah's prophecy had been fulfilled by Jesus' presence and actions, Jesus himself was confessing that he was the long-awaited Messiah. In him all the messianic hopes had been completed. God's kingdom had come (see Luke 11:20; 17:20–21), and "today" (Luke 4:21) was the promised time. In Jesus' sermon in Luke 4, Jesus quoted Isaiah 61:1. He did not, though, quote Isaiah 61:2b, which describes the day of the Lord as a "day of vengeance." Although Israel was hoping the day of the Lord would hold full vengeance for her enemies, Jesus transformed the day into a day that also included grace (see 2 Corinthians 6:2). Jesus made clear that the kingdom was not only something to be looked for in the future, but it *was* already; it *was* at that very time.[18]

Jesus' claim of an already present kingdom was not limited to his sermon in the synagogue at Nazareth. On another occasion, the Pharisees questioned Jesus directly, about "when the kingdom of God was coming" (Luke 17:20). Jesus had already answered this question in the synagogue service (Luke 4). The people, however, had not listened. "The kingdom of God is not coming with signs to be observed," Jesus said, "nor will they say, 'Look, here it is!' or 'There it is!' For behold, the kingdom of God is in your midst" (Luke 4:21).

It was widely believed among Jesus' fellow Jews that when the kingdom of God came the powers of darkness must yield their will to the will of God. The arrival of God's kingdom would be evidenced by the overthrow of all evil powers. Jesus declared, therefore, that his ability to cast out demons with the power of God was a clear indication that the kingdom was already here (Matt. 12:28; Luke 11:20).

The Kingdom Comes Completely

The Jews believed in the doctrine of two ages.[19] This teaching asserted that there was *this age* and *the age to come*. They expected a dramatic close of this age when the new age, the age of the resurrection, began with the coming of God's kingdom.[20]

Jesus, indeed, inaugurated the new age, the age of the resurrection, and, yet, the old age continued. The Jews had never considered this manner of the unfolding of God's activity in history. It seemed strange to them.[21] With the presence of Jesus, the kingdom of God had arrived. Yet, the kingdom was not present in its fullest sense.[22] Paul saw those of us living between the first coming of Jesus and the second as those "upon whom the ends of the ages have come" (1 Cor.10:11). Therefore, we live in a time when the kingdom has already come, but we look forward to its fullness.

While Jesus announced the arrival of the kingdom with his own presence and activity, we also know that Jesus realized the kingdom had not yet fully arrived. Jesus declared that the kingdom had already come. Yet, at the same time, Jesus looked toward a future time, an end time, when the kingdom would come in its greatest power (Matt. 24–25; Mark 13; Luke 21). In this final coming of the kingdom, the Son of Man, Jesus himself, would arrive in complete glory (see Matt. 16:27–28). Even as Jesus taught, "Your kingdom come. Your will be done" (Matt. 6:10), there is a hint of a future fulfillment. Moreover, in Matthew 7:21–23, Jesus referred to "that" day—a day in the future—when commenting on the coming of the kingdom (see also Mark 9:1). Jesus, therefore, could both announce the arrival of God's kingdom and yet expect the final consummation of the kingdom to unfold in future events.

To Call Jesus Lord Is to Call Jesus King

To say "Jesus is Lord" is to say that the kingdom of God has finally arrived. This connection is evident from several New Testament passages, especially in the Book of Acts. Paul's preaching in Ephesus was described as "persuading them about the *kingdom of God*" (Acts 19:8, italics added for emphasis). In this same passage, Luke also described Paul's message as "the word of *the Lord*" (Acts 19:10, italics added for emphasis). Thus, in Ephesus, Paul's "persuading them about the *kingdom of God*" was equal to his teaching about "the word of *the Lord.*" [23] To say "Jesus is Lord" is to say, indeed, that the kingdom has arrived with the new King.

Perhaps the most important passage in Acts regarding the Lordship of Jesus in connection with the kingdom of God is found in the very last depiction of Paul's activity in the book. While Paul was in prison in rented quarters, he welcomed those who came to him. He was "preaching the *kingdom of God* and teaching concerning the *Lord* Jesus Christ . . . " (Acts 28:31, italics added for emphasis). Therefore, to preach about the arrival of the kingdom of God is to teach about the Lordship of Jesus.

The Book of James also contains a connection between the Lord and the kingdom. The author, the brother of Jesus, said that God chose "the poor of this world to be rich in faith and *heirs of the kingdom*" (James 2:5, italics added for emphasis). What kind of faith was it that the members of the kingdom of God were to possess? James has already described believers as those who hold "faith in our glorious *Lord* Jesus Christ" (James 2:1, italics added for emphasis). According to James, therefore, the heirs of the kingdom were those who had called Jesus *Lord*.

So Luke and James connected the Lordship of Jesus with the arrival of the kingdom. Also, Peter described salvation as "entrance into the eternal *kingdom of our Lord* and Savior Jesus Christ" (2 Peter 1:11, italics added for emphasis). Finally, the Apostle John connected the arrival of God's kingdom to both God and "his Christ." The blowing of the seventh trumpet in the Revelation marked the point at which "the kingdom of the world has become *the kingdom of our Lord* and of his Christ; and He will reign for ever and ever" (Revelation 11:15, italics added for emphasis). This passage in Revelation is of particular interest because both God and Christ are linked with the idea of the coming of the kingdom in its fullest and final power.[24]

Conclusion

Like the patient anxiously awaiting the results from an important medical test—a test that could indicate life or death—or the tortured P.O.W. longing for liberation, the ancient Israelites waited for the establishment of God's kingdom. This kingdom was to bring God's rule. God's rule was to be accompanied by a new kind of righteousness among God's people. On the arrival of the kingdom, God's will would finally be accomplished on earth as it already was in heaven.

To say "Jesus is Lord" is to proclaim good news to all who have been looking and longing for God to step into human history. When God's kingdom came, God's people would finally be liberated from the domination of dark powers; the lame would leap; and the blind would see. To call Jesus "Lord" is to say that *the kingdom of God has come into our midst* and yet to know that complete fulfillment lies ahead.

CHAPTER *Four*

Death Is Defeated

To call Jesus Lord
means death is defeated.

STANDING ON THE BEACH AND gazing across the Atlantic Ocean, or staring down from the highest peak of the Rockies to the verdant valley below, or peering up from the bottom of the Grand Canyon, surrounded by soaring walls of earth—all of these privileged positions give one an awe-inspiring view that puts life into a new perspective.

There is another piece of turf where few are allowed to stand. This place will never make anyone else's list of top ten spots for a life-changing view. My life, however, has been radically transformed by standing at the head of hundreds of caskets following a funeral service. From this holy place, I hear the final words of family members as they file by to bid farewell to the one they have loved so deeply. The words that are shared, often whispered in secret, are as varied as the people who share them. But last words are always powerful words.

A man who had been married to his wife for sixty-two years bent over and kissed his lifelong bride farewell. Tears puddled in my eyes as I realized that, despite their countless kisses before, this really was the last one. "Goodbye, sweetie. I love you," he said as he slowly turned toward the door leading to the waiting limousine.

Following another funeral, an elderly woman approached her husband's casket and, in a voice so soft I could barely discern her words, said, "See you after while," as if he were simply running a brief errand to the corner store. She then walked away with courage and confidence.

On another occasion, a daughter, now a young mother in her twenties, approached her father's casket—a father robbed of watching his granddaughter grow as he died a middle-aged man. She said, "Thank you, Daddy," and walked out of the room, weeping.

Many years together—countless conversations—and, in each case, these are the final words, the final farewell. I've witnessed words spoken by those who have confidence in Christ and his resurrection, and I've heard the wavering words of those who have been absolutely devastated by death, devoid of hope. The difference between the demeanor of those who have hope in the resurrection of Christ and those who are forever fearful of death is huge. Those who have called Jesus *Lord* have already overcome death with him. To call Jesus *Lord* is to defeat death.

Introduction

The resurrection, and thus the Lordship of Jesus Christ, is the very center of the Christian faith. So foundational is the idea of the resurrected Christ that Paul said that without it one cannot call oneself a Christian, cannot be a follower of Christ (Romans 10:9).

In the earliest written account in the New Testament of the resurrection, Paul gave us a list of those who saw the resurrected Christ (1 Corinthians 15:3-9). The various Gospel writers reported these first appearances in different ways. John told about Mary Magdalene alone (John 20:11), while Matthew spoke of Mary Magdalene and the other Mary (Matthew 28:1-2). Mark has an account of three women coming to the tomb (Mark 16:1), and Luke seems to imply that a larger company of women came as well (Luke 23:55—24:1, 10).

While some readers are troubled with the imprecision and lack of complete agreement between the various accounts, the truth of the matter is that we find the real authenticity in the variety of the accounts. We may never be certain exactly how many women came when or whether they saw one angelic creature or two. However, the excited and breathless quality of the accounts by the Gospel writers and the lack of intentional harmonizing suggest that the writers did not "doctor" their stories but that they gave the account as they perceived it.

Imagine for a moment ten different witnesses standing at various angles in a bank lobby during a high stakes robbery. Because of different perspectives, focal points, and perceptions, each would tell the story from his or her own experience.

Beware of polished witnesses and harmonized accounts, for therein one may find falsehood.[1] However confusing the resurrection appearances might be to reconstruct in complete detail, there is no confusion over the importance and reality of the resurrection.

The disciples determined that their teacher, Jesus, would initiate the earthly kingdom of God. They even spent time arguing over who would be the greatest when the kingdom actually arrived (Matt. 18:1). Even after Easter, the disciples asked, "Lord, is it at this time You are restoring the Kingdom to Israel?" (Acts 1:6).

They had ushered Jesus into the holy city. As they did, they declared, "Blessed is He who comes in the name of the Lord," in hopes that they were ushering in the kingdom as well (Matt. 21:9).[2] The death of Jesus, however, had shattered all of their hopes and dreams. There was no way, given Jesus' death, that they could continue to cling to the kind of kingdom movement they had created in their minds.[3]

From Discouraged to Daring

Discouraged

Stunned silent described the disciples following the crucifixion of Christ. They thought they were part of a Messianic movement, but some Messiah Jesus had turned out to be. He was crucified, dead, and defeated.

They realized early on that the religious establishment was against this rabbi from Galilee. They even knew that political powers in the Roman regions could brutally put down political and religious uprisings.[4]

But they had followed Jesus for a reason. They had confidence, however slowly it came, that their rabbi was the Christ, the Son of David. They had witnessed him walking on water in the turbulent Sea of Galilee (John 6:16–21) and heard him call his friend Lazarus from the grave (John 11). They had even eaten multiplied loaves and fish (John 6:1–15) and watched as he had driven demons into the depth of the sea (Mark 5:1–13).

The city had been all abuzz just a week earlier as they celebrated Jesus' entrance into Jerusalem as if he were an earthly king. Fickle followers, though, changed their triumphant "Hosanna" to a blood-thirsty "Crucify him!" (Mark 11:10; 15:13). Then the disciples witnessed his body hanging on that awful cross. Beaten and bruised, his broken body was placed, however hurriedly, in a borrowed tomb, wrapped in long strips of cloth as was the traditional custom. Jesus' disciples had committed themselves to following Jesus, and now he was gone. Jesus was dead, his body sealed secure by the powers of Rome. Without Jesus, there was nothing left.[5] Would they again become fishers of fish?

The idea that Jesus might rise from the dead was the furthest thought from the disciples' disappointed minds. In fact, one disciple, the one we call *doubting Thomas*, gained a timeless reputation as a skeptic because he refused to believe in the resurrection until he himself felt the flesh of the crucified Christ (John 20:24–25). As the women reported the resurrection, the men called their breathless babbling about the missing body "nonsense" (Luke 24:11). The Gospels depict the disciples as quaking cowards, hiding behind locked doors, terrified that what had happened to Jesus might happen to them next.[6]

The death of Jesus had shattered all the kingdom hopes of the disciples (Luke 19:11; 24:21). Instead of standing by Jesus, all of the disciples forsook him and fled in fear for their own safety (Mark 14:50). When it came to the crucifixion, Jesus' acquaintances kept their distance (Luke 23:49).[7]

The disciples' discouragement and fear was made all the more evident when none of the Twelve took his body for burial.[8] A member of the Sanhedrin, Joseph, whose position of power perhaps gave him courage, hurriedly buried Jesus (John 19:38).

The disciples were not even the first ones to discover the empty tomb, for they dared not show their faces for fear of losing their own lives. Their hopes for the coming kingdom of God were buried right alongside the body of Jesus.

Jesus had forewarned the disciples about his death (Mark 8:31; 9:12b, 31; 10:33; 14:41c; Luke 17:25) and had even alluded to his resurrection (Matthew 12:40). Even so, the idea that the Messiah, the Deliverer, would end up crucified and cursed on the tree was foreign to any preconceived notion the disciples had of how God would work on behalf of his people (see Luke 18:34).[9] The disciples never expected Jesus' crucifixion. Peter even rebuked his Teacher, the Lord, when Jesus suggested he would suffer (Matt.16:22–23). The people of Jesus' day, including the disciples, could not conceive of the idea that the Messiah would be crucified as a criminal.[10]

Daring

While the disciples were huddled in fear, they were radically transformed from cowards on the run to immovable men who daringly declared that Jesus was alive. Once disillusioned, the disciples began to proclaim boldly the message that even though Jesus had been crucified, God had raised him from the dead (Acts 2:32–36). They asserted that Jesus' death had been the will and the plan of God all along, although it was still a humanly inexcusable murder (Acts 2:23). Peter, who had previously denied even knowing Jesus, was now willing to die to declare Jesus' story (Acts 4:19–20).

How can we explain the disciples' radical transformation from fearful timidity to bold courage? Something clearly happened to convince the disciples that Jesus was alive. They were certain, beyond any doubt, that they had seen him alive, heard his voice, and been comforted by his declaration of peace (John 20:19). The disciples clearly taught and proclaimed that their rabbi and master, whom they had seen crucified, was now alive again.

Despite the fact that their Christ had been crucified, the disciples still announced his messiahship to the Jewish and pagan world. They were willing to redraw their understanding of messiahship around the events that had occurred.[11] There was no other reason for them to persist with such an unexplainable, improbable, and dangerous belief other than that Jesus of Nazareth really was raised from the dead.[12] Although they were surprised by Jesus' resurrection, they accepted it in the face of undeniable evidence. They had been in the presence of the resurrected Christ and understood that through the power of the resurrection, God had demonstrated that Jesus was both the Lord and the Christ (Acts 2:36).

How do you start a new religion with dedicated disciples willing to risk their lives for your message? Fanatical followers and passionate proclaimers are not easily made.

The story is told of a would-be religious leader who was disappointed that his new religion, which he regarded as an improvement on Christianity, had floundered without followers. So, he sought advice. A wise man responded by saying that he did not really know what to do to start a powerful religion, but he knew one plan that seemed to work. He continued, *I recommend that you be crucified and then rise again on the third day.*[13] The wise man recognized that nothing short of an objective, bodily resurrection could create the fearless faith of the once disillusioned disciples.

The Heart of the Matter

Resurrection Is Everything

In spite of what some may say, when we examine the message of the New Testament, especially the preaching of the earliest disciples, we discover that the resurrection of Jesus is absolutely essential to the

Christian faith. At the very heart of the early Christian message we find the declaration that Jesus experienced a bodily resurrection.[14]

New Testament scholar N. T. Wright correctly concluded that while ingenious scholars have invented forms of Christianity that do not hold to the resurrection of Jesus, early Christianity without exception affirmed Jesus' resurrection.[15] As theologian Donald Guthrie affirmed, the resurrection of Jesus is central to New Testament Christianity.[16] New Testament scholar Floyd Filson called the resurrection of Jesus the key fact of the gospel, not just *a* fact.[17]

They Said So in Sermons

The first recorded Christian sermon was the proclamation of the fact that Jesus was now alive (Acts 2:14–36). In this sermon, Peter said very little about the earthly career of Jesus (Acts 2:22). He did not set forth the high ethical demands of the teaching of Jesus, and neither did he spend time arguing about the superiority of Jesus' teachings over those of other rabbis. In fact, he made only passing reference to the mighty deeds that marked Jesus' ministry. Peter's appeal was not, therefore, based on Jesus' incomparable life or outstanding teachings.

What Peter emphasized, however, was that while Jesus had been executed as a criminal, he had experienced the power of God in the resurrection (Acts 2:24–32). He made his appeal based on the fact that God had raised Jesus from the dead and exalted him to God's right hand in heaven. Because of the resurrection, Peter called on ancient Israel to repent (Acts 2:38).

Peter declared, "This Man . . . you nailed to the cross . . . and put Him to death. But God raised Him up again, putting an end to the agony of death since it was impossible for Him to be held in its power" (Acts 2:23b–24). Or again, "This Jesus God raised up again, to which we are all witnesses" (Acts 2:32).

The purpose of the apostles' ministry was not primarily to rule or govern but rather to bear witness to the resurrection of the Lord Jesus (Acts 4:33). When a successor for Judas was selected, the requirement was non-negotiable that the one to replace him must have seen the resurrected Christ personally (Acts 1:22). The apostles were able to do mighty works because God had raised Jesus from the dead (Acts 4:10). Too, it was their incessant declaration of Jesus' bodily resurrection that brought official opposition from the religious leaders (Acts 4:1–2; see 5:30–33). The heart of early Christianity was Jesus' resurrection from the dead.[18]

While other messiahs had come and gone, dying at the hands of a pagan enemy just as Jesus had, their movements either died alongside them or their followers had to rush to center themselves on a new leader. The kingdom movement of Jesus, however, did neither.[19] Unlike any prior messianic movement, within just days of Jesus' execution the movement gained more power and influence than ever before. Despite the cross and the crucifixion, the cause of this Christ did not go away.

How can we explain this unique continuation of the messianic movement of Jesus? The answer of the early Christians was that God had raised Jesus from the dead.[20]

Paul Proclaimed It with His Pen

In the letters of Paul, our earliest New Testament writer, the resurrection of Jesus is interwoven into every aspect of Paul's presentation of Christianity.[21] For example, in one of his letters to the church at Corinth, we see evidence that the resurrection had become part of the earliest Christian tradition. In 1 Corinthians 15, we find a formula that must have been repeated often by the followers of Christ. Here Paul wrote, "For I delivered to you as of first importance what I also received, that Christ died for our sins according to the Scriptures, and that He was buried, and that He was raised on the third day according to the Scriptures" (1 Corinthians 15:3–4).[22] Paul had received this kernel of Christianity and passed it forward to the believers in Corinth. This key summary of the story of Jesus declared both his death, emphasized by the statement of his burial, and his glorious resurrection.

By handing down this early tradition about the death, burial, and resurrection of Jesus, Paul made certain that early Christianity did not consist primarily of a new set of teachings. Rather, it consisted of the announcement of things that had happened, including the Messiah's death and bodily resurrection.

This ancient formula that stressed both the death and the resurrection of Jesus is found throughout the writings of Paul.[23] For example, Paul wrote, ". . . Jesus died and rose again . . . " in his first letter to the church in Thessalonica (1 Thessalonians 4:14). He also wrote, "Christ Jesus is He who died, yes, rather who was raised, who was at the right hand of God" (Romans 8:34). Again he wrote, "For to this end Christ died and lived again, that He might be Lord both of the dead and of the living" (Rom. 14:9). In 2 Corinthians 5:15, Paul called Jesus "[He] . . . who died and rose again. . . ."[24]

So central is the doctrine of the resurrection to Paul's understanding of the story of Jesus that he said we must "confess with [our] mouth Jesus as Lord, and believe in [our] heart[s] that God raised him from the dead" if we hope to experience salvation (Rom. 10:9). To say "Jesus is Lord," therefore, is to believe that God has powerfully, if incomprehensibly, raised Jesus from the dead. Paul was saying that to acknowledge the Lordship of Jesus is to see Jesus in an exalted light and thus to have faith in the risen Lord. Jesus' Lordship makes no sense apart from his resurrection.[25]

Theologian Donald Guthrie concluded that it is reasonable to believe that the term "the Lord" was used of Jesus *only* after his resurrection. New Testament scholar George Ladd confirms this thought, saying, "The title belongs primarily to Jesus as the Risen and Ascended One."[26] Earlier Gospel references to Jesus as the Lord are reflections of the established usage of "the Lord" at the time of writing of the Gospels (which took place, of course, after Jesus' resurrection).

The Resurrection Leads to Recognition of Lordship

Consider some further New Testament evidences that show that Jesus' Lordship is intricately connected to his resurrection. In Luke's Gospel, we find the use of the term "Lord" in a post-resurrection scene in a way that directly unites Lordship and resurrection: "*The Lord* has really *risen*" (Luke 24:34, italics added for emphasis). In the Acts of the Apostles, another work by Luke, the disciples addressed Jesus as the risen Lord after Jesus' resurrection (Acts 1:6). Too, throughout the Book of Acts, the direct prayers of the followers of Christ call on Jesus as Lord (see Acts 1:24; 9:5; 22:8, 19).[27] Resurrection is so connected to Lordship in the New Testament that scholar Marcus Borg wrote, "I see the meanings of Easter as twofold: Jesus lives, and Jesus is Lord."[28]

The Lordship of Jesus is attached not only to his resurrection but also to his exaltation and enthronement to the right hand of God.[29] Jesus is not only alive, but Jesus is also Lord. At the right hand of God, Jesus finds a position of honor, authority, and shared power with the Father. The use of the title *Lord* with Jesus thus refers to the risen, exalted Christ.[30] Recall that it was when Thomas finally saw the resurrected Christ for himself that he declared, "My Lord and my God!" (John 20:28).[31]

Age of the Resurrection

From the time of Ezekiel 37 (sixth century B.C.) onward, the image of resurrection denoted both the return from the exile and the renewal of the covenant. When resurrection occurred, there would be a forgiveness of Israel's sins, because death, in the form of exile, had been dealt with completely. The resurrection, therefore, became a symbol for the new age itself—a central part of the coming kingdom of God. The great patriarchs—Abraham, Isaac, and Jacob—together with all of God's righteous people down through the ages, would be re-embodied and raised to new life in God's new world.[32]

Among the branches of ancient Judaism, the Pharisees, unlike the Sadducees, believed in the resurrection of the body. This bodily resurrection, however, was part of a larger revolution. The arrival of the kingdom of God would bring a new state of affairs on earth in which justice would reign, peace would rule, oppression and wickedness would be defeated, and the righteous dead, who had longed for the coming of the kingdom, would experience a bodily resurrection.[33]

Ancient Israel was not longing and looking for the resurrection of an individual person. Rather, the age of the resurrection would be a part of the great reversal of Israel's bad fortune.[34] Had Jesus simply died and remained dead, the Jews would have concluded that the old age was still present in all of its dark power. On the other hand, when Jesus experienced a bodily resurrection, witnessed by so many, no other conclusion could be drawn than that God's new age had begun.

While mentioned in few Easter sermons, Matthew's account of the resurrection gives us at least an initial hint that, indeed, the resurrection of Jesus had begun the age of the resurrection. In Matthew 27:52–53 we read, "The tombs were opened; and many bodies of the saints who had fallen asleep were raised; and coming out of the tombs after His resurrection, they entered the holy city and appeared to many." When the centurion saw all that had happened with the beginning of the age of the resurrection, he declared, "Truly this was the Son of God!" (Matt. 27:54).

Jesus' resurrection is important not simply because it brought his body back to life.[35] Rather, Jesus' resurrection is especially important because it begins the long-awaited age of the resurrection. Remember, Jesus declared that with him the kingdom had arrived. The Jews understood the arrival of the kingdom of God as including the arrival of the age of the resurrection. With the resurrection of Jesus, the idea of the resurrection of the dead was no longer a distant theological hope for the future. This hope was, indeed, brought into the very present.

So powerful was the resurrection of Jesus that Paul would say that with Jesus' resurrection we, too, had our own resurrection made sure. In a real sense, our resurrection has happened already as we participate in Jesus' resurrection (1 Cor. 15; Rom. 6). The resurrection of Christ and the resurrection of people who belong to Christ are two parts of one whole.[36]

The distance in time between Jesus' resurrection and ours is without importance and does not affect the reality of the relationship between Jesus' resurrection and ours. As Paul said, Jesus is the "first fruits" of the resurrection, and we will be resurrected at "His coming" (1 Corinthians 15:23). His resurrection does not merely give us hope for our resurrection. His resurrection actually *accomplished* our resurrection and inaugurated the age of the resurrection. Just as the first part of the grain harvest indicated that all of the harvest would soon be ripe and gathered in, Jesus' resurrection indicated the certainty that our resurrection would follow. With the resurrection of Christ, the end of the age had finally invaded history.

The irony of the coming of the age of the resurrection was that it happened in a way that no one had ever foreseen. Jesus had begun the age of the resurrection, and yet not all the dead had been raised. The new age had begun but had not come in its fullness. The present age continued, and yet the age of the resurrection had already arrived. Therefore, all that Jesus' followers had learned from the law, the prophets, and the writings of the Old Testament had to be reoriented around the story of Jesus as the new age was unfolded in stages.[37]

But If Not

What if Jesus' body was actually still in the tomb? What if it was suddenly located by an earth-shattering archaeological discovery? Simply put, if the resurrection were a hoax, a tall tale from antiquity, everything else that we have held to be true about Jesus would be proven false and what God was doing in him would be of no effect.[38]

Pointing to the crucifixion alone as the central event of the Christ story misses the mark. While the crucifixion is of prime importance, without the resurrection the crucifixion nullifies Jesus' claim to be the Christ. The first-century Jew would not have been impressed by Jesus' crucifixion. On the contrary, the very fact that Jesus was crucified would have meant that Jesus was *not* the true Messiah and that the kingdom had not come.[39]

Paul himself took up the task of pretending there was no resurrection (1 Cor. 15). Without the actual resurrection, Paul said: (1) the preaching of the gospel is in vain; (2) our faith is in vain; (3) we are liars because we have testified that God has raised Jesus; (4) we have not been forgiven of our sins; (5) those who have died with false hope in Christ have simply perished forever; and (6) we are a pitiful people who have placed our hope in a helpless Christ (1 Cor. 15:12–19). Paul was asserting that if you take away the resurrection, the whole message of the gospel unravels in your very hands.[40]

Without the resurrection, Jesus remains little more than a curious enigma. Perhaps he was a good teacher, a powerful leader, or maybe even a wise man of prayer. Without the resurrection, though, Jesus was clearly a failure. With the resurrection, however, Jesus has achieved victory over evil and death to the very ends of the cosmos.[41]

William James (1842-1910), the psychologist and philosopher, reasoned that if we were a part of a universe in which Jesus could be murdered and not resurrected, then depression and defeat would be the only attitudes that made sense. The only real event in history that gives us hope is the resurrection of Jesus. As Morton Kelsey, the Episcopalian author on spirituality, wrote, "Allowing the resurrected One to be constantly present, I can deal with all the evil suffered by Jesus, by my friends, and by me. . . . The resurrection reveals the ultimate nature of the universe, and the risen Christ continues to give victory over the power of evil."[42]

Conclusion

The resurrection of Jesus is not only the foundation for the future hope of Christians but also the center of our present hope as well. With Jesus' resurrection, we no longer have to be afraid of the ultimate enemy, death. In fact, Paul boldly claimed that death itself will be defeated (1 Cor. 15:26). With the resurrection of Jesus, death has lost its "sting" (1 Cor. 15:55), and we find ourselves swept up in the victory of Christ. Therefore, we are to be "steadfast, immovable, always abounding in the work of the Lord, knowing that your toil is not in vain in the Lord" (1 Cor. 15:58).

God has the last word in Christ's resurrection, and the last word is life, not death. Light, not darkness. Victory, not defeat. We find the supreme display of cosmic power in the empty tomb. Corruption, decay, and death have been checked. By raising his own Son from the dead, God has provided a way of life for all who follow him. Because the early Christians understood resurrection hope, their funerals were celebrations, and those in attendance wore white.[43]

I recently conducted the funeral of Raymond Andrews, who died at ninety-seven years of age. He and his bride, Mary Mildred Vineyard, who was of equal age, had been married for seventy-three-and-a-half years. She recalled how they had met while both were attending Hardin-Simmons University in Abilene, Texas. He just happened to be coming out of a café near the school while she was going in. Frank, Raymond's brother, introduced the two of them. The very next day, Raymond called Mary Mildred.

With the Depression on the American horizon, the date consisted of little more than sitting on a bench on the Hardin-Simmons campus and chatting. No one had money for a date during those lean days. They quickly fell in love and were soon engaged to be married. Although they longed to be married, they were afraid that, due to the Depression, marriage might mean starvation. After their love had held on as long as it could, they finally decided they would "just get married and starve to death together," Mary Mildred said, with a chuckle in her voice and a twinkle in her eye.

When I showed excitement over their seventy-three plus years of marriage, she seemed to push it aside. "Oh, after seventy-three-and-a-half years, I was just getting acquainted with Raymond, and the Lord came and took him away!"

Yes, the Lord did take him away, but just for a while. For on the great day of the resurrection, Mr. Andrews and Mrs. Andrews will be reunited in the community of Christ. Because of the resurrection, we can smile at Raymond's funeral, take hope in Christ's provision of salvation, and long for the day of reunion.

CHAPTER *Five*
A New Family Is Formed

To call Jesus Lord *means Jesus'*
followers belong to a new family.

A MOTHER FRANTICALLY TRIED TO AWAKEN her son. "Get up, son. Today is Sunday. Sunday School begins at 9:30."

"I know, Mother, but I'm not going today."

"Why not?" she inquired.

"I'll give you two reasons," he replied. "First, I don't feel like getting up this morning. Second, no one down at the church likes me. Everyone is against me."

But the mother persisted in trying to awaken her son. "But you've got to get out of bed. And I'll give you two reasons why. First of all, you're twenty-nine years old. And second, you're the pastor of the church!"

There are times when none of us feels like going to church—even pastors. But when we call Jesus *Lord*, we are entering into a family. To call Jesus *Lord* is to take on the community responsibility of belonging to the people of God (Ephesians 2:11–19). You cannot be a committed follower of Christ on the one hand and not a committed church member on the other. Being a Christian disciple and belonging to a church go together.

Sheep Without a Flock

Some families who consider themselves Christian never actually belong to one church. Rather, they pick and choose from the menu of ministries from two or more churches. On the weekend, they attend the church that has "exciting worship." On Wednesday evenings, however, they drop the children off at the more traditional church where outstanding children's programs are offered.

Our culture, moreover, promotes individual spirituality. This type of renegade religion concludes that an individual's relationship with God is no one else's concern and a person's spiritual relationship is with the Creator and not with a community. As a result of the proliferation of personalized religion, many more people claim to be followers of Jesus than those who actually gather with Jesus' people to celebrate on Sunday—Jesus' resurrection day. According to a recent study by the Barna Group, sixty-two percent of the seventy-six million adults who have not attended any type of church in the past six months actually claim to be followers of Christ.[1] In another study, only eighteen percent of the adults surveyed believe that "spiritual maturity requires involvement in a community of faith."[2]

For a myriad of reasons, people neglect gathering to worship God (Hebrews 10:25). Some should-be worshipers have been burned by bad experiences. Others claim they get nothing out of church. Still others declare they are turned off by the hypocrites they find in the house of God. Soccer fields and baseball diamonds draw other believers away from the culture of Christ into the worship of sports endeavors. Little League disciples and sport devotees leave others behind to worship God while they worship getting a goal or hitting a home run. Shoppers, meanwhile, crowd the malls on Sunday—the modern cathedrals of a consumer culture. The weary seek Sunday sleep and slumber, and the workaholic refuses to stop and reflect (Psalm 46:10) even when God himself rested and required God's people to set aside a holy Sabbath (Exodus 20:10).

Forsaking the community is unacceptable, however, because to say "Jesus is Lord" is to say *you and I are family, brothers and sisters.* The call of the New Testament is not to become an individual follower of

Jesus, standing alone. The call, rather, is to enter a community. Jesus invites us to become part of God's people, God's family. We restore our relationship with God as we believe in the story of Jesus and become part of God's covenant people. Through our faith in Christ, represented by our obedience in baptism, we are incorporated into the body of God's people. Baptism is the initiation into a new culture, a culture that we call *the church*.[3]

Belonging to the Family

A few years ago, a visitor to our church completed a visitor's registration slip in Sunday School. She stated her name, address, telephone number, and continued to fill out the form. Nothing unusual so far. The next question was, "Are you a Christian?" "Yes," she answered. The question that followed was "Are you a church member?" to which she candidly replied, "Little bit."

When I received this visitor's card the following Monday, I couldn't help but chuckle, appreciating her honesty and yet disagreeing with her theology. To call Jesus *Lord* is to accept an invitation into the family of God. We are never called to be a "little bit" connected to our brothers and sisters in Christ. We are, on the contrary, called to be committed to community.

By definition, being a Christian is belonging to a community. We become part of the story of ancient Israel, a peculiar people represented by the church.[4] In Galatians 3:29 we read, "And if you belong to Christ, then you are Abraham's offspring, heirs according to promise." We are bound to one another by our common faith in our Lord. As we enter into a covenant with Christ, we simultaneously enter into a covenant of caring for and accountability to Christ's other followers.

The story of God's people has always been a story about families. We begin with the story of Adam and his family—one good son and one bad (Genesis 4). Noah's family follows (Gen. 6—9), and Abraham's family is extended through the stories of Isaac and Jacob (Gen. 12—50).

The image of God's people in the New Testament builds on this Old Testament emphasis on family.[5] As followers of Christ, we are adopted into God's family (Rom. 8:15, 17; Galatians 3:26—4:7). Thus, as we share adoption into the family of God, we become brothers and sisters. Like children chosen from an orphanage, we take on a new parent, new siblings, new names, and a new inheritance (Gal. 3:29).[6] We share our common Father, God, and inherit freedom from the powers of sin and death. Jesus himself saw us as his family as we walk in covenant obedience: "For whoever does the will of My Father who is in heaven, he is My brother and sister and mother" (Matthew 12:50).

Paul told Timothy to treat older men as if they were his father and younger men as if they were his brothers. Older women in the church were to be as mothers to Timothy while younger women were to be as his sisters (1 Timothy 5:1-2). Paul depicted himself as "mother" and "father" (1 Thessalonians 2:7, 11) and thus gave the Thessalonians the status of children in God's family.

In the New Testament, Christians are depicted as loving, as loving brothers and sisters love each other.[7] The New Testament applies language that was commonly used to describe the love shared in a biological family to the love experienced among God's people: "Now as to the *love of the brethren*, you have no need for anyone to write to you, for you yourselves are taught by God to love one another" (1 Thess. 4:9, italics added for emphasis). The idea of believers sharing the love of a family is commonplace in the New Testament (Rom. 12:10; Heb. 13:1; 1 Peter 1:22; 2 Peter 1:7).

A prospective deacon in our church was sharing his testimony as part of the process moving toward ordination. This particular young man had lost his father at an early age. He looked at his church family and declared, "When I needed a father, you were my fathers. When I needed a mother, you were my mothers. I needed a brother, and you were my brothers. I needed sisters, and you were by my side."

God's people are always and everywhere in the New Testament to love one another like family. The New Testament witness that we should see one another as siblings is strong. Indeed, it is so strong that John concluded that we cannot love God, whom we have not seen, if we do not love our brothers and sisters whom we *have* seen. Loving one's brothers and sisters is an essential element of loving God (1 John 4:20-21). This family-like love among God's people happens in the setting of a local church.

The Gathered People of God

The New Testament Greek word for church, *ekklesia*, came to Paul from the Greek Old Testament, the Septuagint. In the Greek Old Testament, the *ekklesia* was none other than the congregation of Israel, especially as they assembled before the Lord at Mount Sinai (or Mount Horeb) to hear his word (Exodus 19:1–2; Deuteronomy 1:6). Because Paul used such a vivid image for the new community centered on the crucified and risen Lord, we understand a lot about what Paul was saying about the nature and importance of the Christian community.[8] Paul's other images that depict the church also set forth the premier importance of God's gathered people: the bride of Christ (Eph. 5:25); the body of Christ (Eph. 4:12); the new Israel or the people of God (Eph. 2:12–13; 1 Peter 2:10); the household or family of God (Eph. 2:19; 3:15); and the planting of God to bring forth fruit to God's glory (1 Corinthians 3:8–9; John 15:1–8).

Each local church represents the covenant people of God. The New Testament, in fact, most often applies the word *ekklesia*, translated *church*, to a local group of baptized believers.[9] For example, Paul often wrote something like this: *Paul, an apostle of Christ Jesus, to the church in. . . .* Then he would name the city to which he was writing (see 1 Cor. 1:2; 1 Thess. 1:1). In the Acts of the Apostles, the local church developed as an expression of commitment to Christ. We read about the local church in Jerusalem (Acts 15), in Antioch (13:1), and in Caesarea (18:22). In the Book of Revelation, we learn about the seven letters to local churches (Revelation 2—3). There are no *lone ranger* Christians in the New Testament. Rather, people who follow Christ are part of a localized body of Christ.

The local church is as much a part of the teaching of the New Testament as the deity of Christ or the creative powers of God. Calling into question the validity of the local church would also call into question the entire revelation of the New Testament. To say belonging to and participating in a church is not important is the equivalent of saying that discipleship is not important, for in Scripture they are one and the same.

The notion that *church* can exist without a local expression is without merit. The larger idea of church makes sense only when there is also a local group of believers to embody that idea. The New Testament is clear that churches were organized bodies and not temporary or loose groupings of individuals. The church at Antioch, for example, had much more than a passing purpose. The churches at Rome, Corinth, Philippi, and Thessalonica were permanent and definitely organized bodies.

The church is called to fulfill its Christ-given agenda, the evangelization of the world. We are commanded to go, make disciples, baptize them, and teach them (Matthew 28:18–20). Believers everywhere have organized in order to fulfill the commands of Christ's commission.

Christ and the Church

Words That Link

Jesus believed that the church was closely connected to him. According to Matthew's Gospel, Jesus said, "I will build *My* church" (16:18, italics added for emphasis). The connection between the church and Christ is made even more evident, however, in the writings of Paul.[10] At times, Paul almost identifies Christ with the church. This super-identification occurs as the church and Christ undergo suffering together, hold a shared unity, and experience a common resurrection.

First, to persecute the church is to persecute Christ. The church is so connected to Christ that on the road to Damascus, as Paul was persecuting the church, the resurrected Christ asked, "Why are you persecuting *Me*? . . . I am Jesus whom you are persecuting" (Acts 9:4–5, italics added for emphasis). Paul's inflicting suffering on the church was equivalent to causing Christ to suffer. The church is, after all, the body of Christ (Rom. 12:4–5; 1 Cor. 12:27).

Second, we can also see the close connection between Christ and the church when we learn that to divide the church is to divide Christ. The church in Corinth was split into four parties—the party of Paul, the party of Apollos, the party of Cephas, and the party of Christ (1 Cor. 1:12–13). Although it was the church that was divided,

Paul wrote, "Has *Christ* been divided?" (1 Cor. 1:13, italics added for emphasis). Later in this letter, as he described the variety of gifts found within the church, Paul used the image of the human body. There is a variety of members of the human body—eye, foot, hand, etc.—and yet only one body. Paul then wrote, "So also is *Christ*" (1 Cor. 12:12, italics added for emphasis), when we expect him to write *church*. The church is so connected to Christ that sometimes Paul used the words interchangeably! To be in Christ is to be in the church.

The church, third, participates in the age of the resurrection, which has begun already in the resurrection of Christ (Rom. 6:3–8; 2 Cor. 5:17). Among the things shared in common by those who gather to worship the risen Lord is the certain eternal future that they experience with him. Paul wanted the church to know the resurrection power by which Jesus was both raised and exalted to God's right hand (Eph. 1:19–23). We have, in fact, already been raised up "with Him" (Eph. 2:6).

Images That Link

The church is also depicted as inextricably linked to Christ in images from Paul's letters. For example, the church is the temple (1 Cor. 3:16–17; Eph. 2:19–22). As the temple, the church is the spiritual environment where God is rightly worshiped. The church is the place for the indwelling presence of the Spirit of the risen Lord.[11] As the bride of Christ, moreover, the church is called to be holy and pure as an indication of "her" devotion to Christ (2 Cor. 11:2; 6:16). The images of the church as the temple of the exalted Lord and the bride of Christ place the church in the closest position alongside our Lord.

The Church and the Kingdom of God

To say "Jesus is Lord" is to say the kingdom of God has arrived (see chapter 3). The church, however, cannot be completely identified with the kingdom of God. The church is a gathering of those who have accepted the arrival of the King and his kingdom, becoming joint heirs of that kingdom.[12]

Jesus, for example, does not actually regard his disciples as constituting the kingdom. Jesus himself, rather, represented the kingly rule of God on earth (Luke 11:20). The kingdom centers, therefore, on Christ and not the disciples. A community develops, however, among those who are willing to allow the rule of God to dominate their lives under the Lordship of Jesus.[13] Jesus even speaks of *entering* the kingdom when referring to belonging to the covenant people who celebrate God's rule and reign in both heaven and earth (Matt. 7:21; Mark 9:47; see Luke 16:16).

Church Shopping and Hopping

The pastor of a Baptist church in Florida created a "compact, mini 22-minute worship service." In his 1,320-second service, the pastor delivers an eight-minute sermon, leads in the singing of one hymn, reads Scripture, and offers a prayer. His logic is this: "It's for people whose parents made them go to church all their lives, and they thought they had all the church they could stand. Or, it's a good entry-level church for people to see if they can take religion in smaller doses."[14]

This approach might seem to be a creative way to reach the unchurched. However, I am afraid that the pastor's mini-worship service is indicative of a broader movement to create an entertaining, self-centered atmosphere rather than a call to servanthood among the people of God.

I received a promotional piece for a new church in our community. The promotional piece boldly declared that their services would "always be casual, always contemporary, always laughter"—and they would skip the "sermons" to have "conversational teaching." Last, but not least, they would "always finish early so you can get on with your day." The brochure promised that their worship service would be something like "sitting through a Seinfeld episode" rather than sitting through traditional worship. They promised that their multimedia presentations would make the "Titanic look cheesy." Although the intentions might be good, the result seems to water down the requirements and dilute the demands of Christianity in order to draw a crowd.

Many people with a consumer mentality ponder all the wrong questions as they visit churches:

- Will the sermon be entertaining and make me feel good about myself?
- Are the staff members in the student ministry "cool" enough to hold the attention of my teenager?
- Is the music powerful, moving, and enjoyable?
- Does the church have my favorite ministry or program on its menu of ministries?

Today's churchgoer begins the search for a church pondering, *What can this church do for me?* Of course, the problem with the consumer mentality toward church is that it operates from the wrong perspective. We are not getting good answers because we are asking the wrong questions. The only question that matters is this: *Has God been pleased with the sacrifice of worship and service from his people?*

When we arrive at church seeing the pastor and minister of worship as entertainers on a theater stage, we miss the meaning of what God has called us to experience. Acting as a theater critic—judging the sermon and grading the music—we rob ourselves of a holy encounter. God is interested in the sacrifice of our hearts, an internal attitude of submission and thanksgiving for all that God has done for his people through the story of Jesus.[15] In reality, the pastor and worship leaders are the prompters. The congregation consists of the actors, and God is the only audience that counts.

When we gather to worship God, we should join the prophet Isaiah as he encountered a righteous God and declared, "Holy, Holy, Holy" (Isa. 6:3). Our worship must offer more than theology that can be summarized on bumper stickers and t-shirts. As we pattern our worship after Isaiah 6, we follow our encounter with a holy God with the recognition of our sinfulness and the declaration of our willingness to serve, once cleansed. With the prophet Isaiah, we say, "Here am I. Send me" (Isa. 6:8).

Beyond Self to Service

The New Testament church offers more than a baptized version of feel-good pop psychology that promises to help us deal with our depression and succeed over our stress. The gospel contains more than instruction about parenting or supportive suggestions that help us deal with our difficult past. Historic Christianity proclaims the earth-shattering message that the Messiah has arrived in the person of Jesus Christ. It proclaims that somehow God was at work in Jesus' death and resurrection in such a way that our sins have been forgiven and our eternity made secure as we both die and live with him.

Every pastor is tempted to dilute this message, to rush people down the aisle, and to make it all easy and entertaining. But to do so is to miss the mark regarding how Jesus called his disciples. When challenging the rich young ruler to sell all of his possessions and give the proceeds to the poor, Jesus was demanding unconditional allegiance and commitment (Matt. 19:16–30; Mark 10:17–31; Luke 18:18–25). Jesus first tested his followers before he allowed them to walk in his footsteps. Christ called his followers to a costly discipleship, and only to that. German theologian Dietrich Bonhoeffer prophetically declared,

> Cheap grace is the deadly enemy of our Church. We are fighting today for costly grace.

> Cheap grace is the preaching of forgiveness without requiring repentance, baptism without church discipline, Communion without confession, absolution without personal confession. Cheap grace is grace without discipleship. . . .
> Costly grace is the treasure hidden in the field; for the sake of it a man will gladly go and sell all that he has. It is the pearl of great price to buy which the merchant will sell all his goods. . . . It is the call of Jesus Christ at which the disciple leaves his nets and follows him.[16]

The church must be more than a vendor of various religious goods and services that seeks only to gain and retain more members with the latest menu of ministries.[17] We must go on mission to make disciples, to serve others. We must understand ourselves as called and sent by the God of the Good News. The church must focus more on its God-given mission to others and less on amusing itself. We are called as a church to reach out to a decaying and dying world, carrying the hope-filled message of the Christ. We gather for worship, and we scatter for service.

Power Among God's People

When God's people gather as a church, much more is accomplished than arriving at the simple sum total of individuals and their abilities. As those called to be part of God's people gather as one body, something new, far beyond a collection of faltering individuals, is created. Within the church, we find encouragement and support for the journey of faith, are held accountable for our actions and beliefs, and exercise our spiritual gifts to build up God's people.

Support from Community

None of us can lead a life of faith alone. An often repeated folk story tells about a man who had stopped going to church, although he had been a regular and faithful attender. After he had missed three weeks in a row, the pastor decided it was time to pay him a visit. The evening was chilly, and the pastor found the man at home alone, sitting before a blazing fire.

Guessing the reason for the pastor's visit, the man sheepishly welcomed him, led him to a big chair in front of the fireplace, and waited to be chided. The pastor made himself comfortable but didn't say anything. Amidst the long, awkward silence, the pastor watched the play of the flames around the burning logs. After a few minutes, the pastor left his chair, took the fire tongs, and carefully picked up a brightly burning ember. He placed it to the side of the hearth—all alone, by itself. Then he sat back in his chair, still and silent.

The host watched all this in quiet fascination. As the one lone ember's flame diminished, there was a momentary glow, and then its orange fire turned black as coal.

Not a word had been spoken since the initial greeting. Just before the pastor was ready to leave, he picked up the cold, dead ember and placed it back in the middle of the blazing fire. Immediately it began to glow again, emitting light and warmth like the surrounding coals. As the pastor reached the door to leave, his host said, "Thank you so much for your visit. I'll see you back in church next Sunday."

We all need a place where we belong and find the support of fellow believers. We are to "bear one another's burdens" (Gal. 6:2) and to "encourage the fainthearted" (1 Thess. 5:14). As Philip Yancey, author of bestselling Christian books, wrote, "Everyone who returns from a long and difficult trip is looking for someone waiting for him at the station or the airport. Everyone wants to tell his story and share his moments of pain and exhilaration with someone who stayed home, waiting for him to come back."[18] At church, fellow believers are waiting to see us.

A therapist listens to us because we pay for the therapist's services. The store clerk smiles because he or she is trained in customer service. The nurse changes the dressing of our wound because it is hospital procedure. All of these are honorable endeavors and practices, to be sure. But in the community of Christ, people serve one another simply because they carry the love of Christ in their hearts.[19]

Boundaries for Belief and Behavior

Without a community, we are each left to our own individual spirituality, adrift on a sea of subjectivity. To try to interpret the Bible apart from a church, apart from a community, amounts to no less than each reader creating his or her own individual religion. In church, we listen to the testimony of the saints and hear the ancient words of faith. We are guided, challenged, and called to walk a common path. Scriptures were written for churches. Remember, Paul began his letters, "Paul . . . to the church in. . . ." What Paul wrote was to be read and reasoned among the gathered people of God.

We also find within the church boundaries for our behavior. Jesus himself described the process of restoring a fellow believer back into the family of faith. If the offending believer will not respond to your personal pleas or to a limited number of witnesses, then you are to bring the matter before the church (Matt. 18:17). Church discipline was pursued when an individual's sin threatened to unravel the fabric of the family of God. In Corinth, the issue surrounded a man who was sleeping with "his father's wife," his stepmother (1 Cor. 5:1). In Thessalonica, the problem was the sin of laziness (2 Thess. 3:6–12). In both cases, the church exercised discipline when the behavior of an individual within the church was threatening the unity and effectiveness of the church as a whole. The goal of the discipline, however, in both cases was to protect the church and restore the offending member back into the body of believers.

Building Up the Body

Each member of the body of Christ is equipped with spiritual gifts. As the hand, eye, and foot combine their abilities with other members to create a functioning human body, so also each member of the church uses his or her gift with the gifts of others to form a single body of faith. No gift was to be considered more important than another. For Paul, the gifts were always to be exercised so as to build up the body (1 Cor. 12). In God's choir, no one sings solo! We are all called to harness our gifts with the gifts of other members to create a melody of praise. Paul wrote, ". . . since you are zealous of spiritual gifts, seek to abound for the edification of the church" (1 Cor. 14:12).

A Place for Everybody

Church should be the one place on earth where everyone feels equal and everyone is treated the same. In the Book of James, we are told we should not judge people by appearance. We should not be prejudiced.

Our Lord's brother said that if we give the rich the seat of honor while pushing the poor to the floor, then we have played favorites (James 2:1-3). We should not honor the rich and disgrace the poor. Church ought to be the one place on earth where everyone, rich or poor, should feel as if he or she has a place among all the people of God.

We are never to approach the place of worship like the haughty Pharisee, but rather we are to come as the humble sinner, barely lifting our eyes to heaven (Luke 18:13). Church is the one place where we gather with people of various political persuasions, generations, and cultural backgrounds—all committed to a common Christ.

Fred Craddock, the renowned preacher and teacher of preaching, remembers growing up poor when his family had lost their farm. As they gathered together in the fall on the first day of school, all the children were sharing their summer vacations as an icebreaker. One student had been to Florida; another to Niagara Falls; and another to Washington to experience all the historic monuments. Saved by the bell, Craddock went home downcast because he was going to have to share his summer vacation on the next day. He had only worked on the farm all summer.

His father encouraged him to weave a tale from the best parts of other students' stories because it wouldn't be appropriate to say he had done nothing but hoe sweet potatoes all summer long. The truth was Craddock felt like a nobody because he had gone nowhere and had nothing to share.

With some guilt and under compulsion from his father, Craddock started to "tie them on. 'I went up to New York and Washington. . . .' I was somewhere on this side of Niagara Falls when the teacher called me into the hall and said, 'You didn't do all that.'"

"No, ma'am."

"Well, why did you say all that?"

"Because I was embarrassed."

"Why were you embarrassed?"

"Because I worked on the farm all summer long."

He remembers it was not a bad summer. He wished he had told the truth and said that he had thrown sweet potatoes at a squirrel and knocked the squirrel off a limb, and that he had kept his sister screaming by tossing the potatoes her way.

One day a group of women from the Central Avenue Christian Church in Humboldt, Tennessee, visited the Craddock home. They brought things for the children to wear, and among them was a pair of shoes that were just Fred's size.

"Good," Fred's mother said, "now you can go to Sunday School." Craddock later learned they were girls' shoes, but it did not matter at the moment. He didn't want to go to Sunday School because he figured it would be the same. People would ask, *What did you do on vacation? Who are you and how much do you have?* But from the first day, wearing those charity shoes, Fred Craddock found out that church was a different kind of place. "I was never, ever embarrassed in church. I don't remember ever feeling any different, any less, any more, any different from anybody else in church. And from the age of nine until now, I have had this little jubilee going on in my mind: There is no place in the world like church."[20]

Church must be the one place where money is not the measure, where skin color counts for nothing, and where political power is pointless. Among God's people there is neither Jew nor Gentile, slave nor free, male nor female (Gal. 3:28).

Conclusion

To call Jesus *Lord* is to commit to community and to gathering with God's missional people. Even our faithful weekly worship—skipping Sunday soccer games and missing the mall until Monday—is a testimony in itself. Sunday is different for God's people, for it is the day that the Lord Jesus Christ defeated death. On that day, the early followers of Christ Jesus discovered they had, indeed, been following the Lord all along, the one who would be exalted to the right hand of God.

Something is taking place in your local community of worship that is too important for you to miss. There, the eternal touches the temporal.

A young woman, twenty-eight years of age, said to the preacher as she was leaving a church, "This is the first time I was ever in a church."

"Really?"

"Yeah."

"Well, how was it?"

"Kind of scary," she replied.

"Kind of scary?"

"Yeah."

"Why?"

"It just seems so important," she said. "You know, I never go to anything important. This just seemed so important."[21]

In Thornton Wilder's classic play, *Our Town*, are these important lines:

> *Everyone knows in their bones that something is eternal, and that something has to do with human beings. All the greatest people ever lived have been telling us that for five thousand years and yet you'd be surprised how people are always losing hold of it. There's something way down deep that's eternal about every human being.*[22]

In our deepest selves, we intuitively know that there must be more to our existence than seventy-five-plus-or-less earthly years. We come to church each week because we know that there is indeed more. There is more to life than gathering material things. There is more that counts than our daily jobs. We worship with a sense of hope for more. As we praise God, we search for meaning. Our Creator alone gives us the answer to these larger than life questions.

Sometimes the hymns may be mundane, and the preacher may be doing less than waxing eloquently. Nonetheless, in the midst of what may seem to be mediocrity, we still encounter a holy God.

Of course, the church today, just like the church of the New Testament, is full of blunders and bloopers because even though we follow Christ we have clay feet. While the church often falters and fails, you must remember that like a high school orchestra struggling to play Beethoven's "Ninth Symphony," we are trying our best to be the people of God. Sometimes it sounds good just to hear somebody trying to play the piece written by the master.

A preacher and scholar remembered that his mother took him to Sunday School every Sunday, but his father never accompanied the family. Rather, his father would stay home and complain when the Sunday dinner was late. The preacher would call, and his father would always say, "That church doesn't care about me; all that church wants is another pledge and another name, another pledge and another name. That's what church is all about."

Sometimes when an evangelist would come through to do revivals, the pastor would bring the evangelist over and say, *Sic him*, but nobody was ever able to get to his father, for he had a cold, cold heart. "The church doesn't care about me," his father always said.

The son said, "I heard my father say, 'All they want is another name and another pledge,' more than a thousand times."

But there was one day he didn't say it. He was in the hospital, and he was down to seventy-three pounds. They had taken out his throat and said, "It's too late." They had put in a metal tube, and X-rays had burned him to pieces. The son flew in to see his dying father who, by now, could not speak and could not even eat.

Around the room were potted plants and cut flowers. They were sitting on all the window sills. Stacks of cards two feet tall covered the food tray. Every card and every blossom represented a person or a group from the church that his father had never acknowledged.

The son picked up one of the cards and read it. His father, who could not speak, reached for a tissue box and wrote on the side a line from Shakespeare. "In this harsh world, draw your breath in pain to tell my story."[23]

"What is your story, Daddy?"

"And he wrote, 'I was wrong.'"[24]

If we miss the church as the people of God, as the covenant community of the Lord, then we will be wrong, too. To follow Christ is to gather with his people. People go to church for a myriad of reasons. Some go to be seen. Others go to find hope. Some are certain there is a God who keeps track, and they want to stay on God's good side. Some go trying to find a salve for their anxiety, and others daydream of other places while they sit in the pew. But we all go with a sense of hope—hope of encountering a holy and righteous God so that this God can change our lives through his Son.

CHAPTER Six
We Are to Live Jesus' Way

To call Jesus Lord *means we
are to live Jesus' way.*

WHEN WE CALL JESUS LORD, we commit ourselves to following our sinless Savior. We reorient our core values to Jesus' kingdom values.

While we find forgiveness in Jesus' Lordship, Christianity is no license to sin freely. Paul wrote, "Are we to continue in sin that grace might increase? May it never be! How shall we who died to sin still live in it?" (Romans 6:1b–2). We are not to take God's grace lightly or trample on it. Knowing the call of Christ on our lives and the example of Christ's obedience, surely we can conclude that we who claim to have committed ourselves to Christ are to live by unique moral standards—standards that are different from those who do *not* call him *Lord*.

When we examine the evidence, however, we discover that we often fail to follow Jesus. Christians frequently seem to walk just as the world walks. Christians may claim Jesus as Lord with their words, but their actions show that their real commitments are to money, sex, and personal fulfillment.[1] It may well be that Christians have done so poorly in living up to the words "Jesus is Lord" that few people know what such a commitment really means.[2]

How condemning is the evidence? How far have we faltered?

Various surveys by pollsters Gallup and Barna lead to the conclusion that the lifestyle of many Christians tends to be little different from that of the world in general.[3] We Christians seem to divorce our spouses, live in materialistic luxury, and judge people by the color of their skin just as our pagan neighbors do.

Instead of maintaining Christian distinctives, the church is becoming more like secular society. Pollster George Barna concluded that the church in America is currently being affected by the surrounding culture rather than having any influence on society.[4]

No area of life is excluded from Jesus' Lordship. While space will not permit us to address every area of behavior, several concrete examples demonstrate that Christians have failed to live like Christ. Our relationship with the material world and our human relationships demonstrate that we have not translated the words of Christ into our everyday lives.

Given to Gold

John and Roberta were touring their brand new house. Roberta had paid for the house with her money, a fact of which she constantly reminded John. In each room of the house, she said to her husband: "John, if it were not for my money, we would not be here." John did not say a word.

That afternoon, a truck delivered a load of new furniture—furniture that Roberta paid for with her money. After the furniture was in its place, they toured the house again. As they observed each room, beautifully appointed and magnificently decorated, Roberta reminded her husband, "John, if it were not for my money, this furniture would not be here." Again, John was silent.

Late in the afternoon, another truck arrived with a special piece of furniture which was to be the focal point of the family room. It was a combination stereo-television-computer center all wrapped into one gorgeous piece of furniture. Roberta, of course, paid for it with her money. When it was proudly in place, Roberta again said: "John, if it were not for my money, that beautiful electronics system would not be here."

Finally, John spoke: "Honey, I don't want to make you feel bad, but, if it were not for your money, I wouldn't be here either!"[5]

If we are honest with ourselves, we have to admit that many Christians in the consumer-driven culture of America live as materialistically as their unbelieving neighbors. Our cars are just as luxurious, our homes just as grand, and our possessions just as plentiful. Like John, we go after the gold. C. S. Lewis noted, "Prosperity knits a man to the World. He feels that he is 'finding his place in it,' while really it is finding its place in him."[6]

Stuff to Store

Someone once said that clutter consists of things that are worth saving that haven't been put away, deposited on top of things that are not worth saving but haven't been thrown away, which have settled next to things you aren't sure what to do with.

The last time I moved, I couldn't believe the number of boxes. Two hundred and forty was the official count from the moving company. If you have not moved within the last two years, you have no idea just how many boxes it would take to transport your household to a new city. I remember one box. The contents were simply labeled "Stuff." S-T-U-F-F.

It was neither a blender nor a lamp—just *stuff*, that indescribable collection of American paraphernalia properly called *stuff*. We have so much stuff as Americans that we buy little metal buildings to go into our backyards to store our extra stuff. Container stores now exist just so we can organize our stuff for storage.

We cut holes in our hallways so we can pull down a secret set of stairs and cram that space between our roof and our ceiling with stuff. If someone cleans out the garage, we ask, *Hey, what did you do with my stuff?*

Occasionally, when we cannot possibly put another thing in our storage closets, we have a *stuff sale* on Saturday, and others come and take our stuff away to place in their storage. If the sale starts at 9 o'clock in the morning, eager buyers will show up at 7 o'clock because they don't want all the good stuff to be gone. After the stuff sale, we brag, *I made $350 today!* We forget that we paid $2,750 retail for the same stuff.

Having cleaned a closet, we say, *Hey, neat. Look. I forgot I had all this stuff.* You can even rent some space by the month in which to put your extra stuff.

Then we die, and an auctioneer sells all of our stuff to the highest bidder.

In an insightful book, John DeGraaf, David Wann, and Thomas H. Naylor have described the current American epidemic of accumulating stuff as "affluenza—a painful, contagious, socially transmitted condition of overload, debt, anxiety, and waste resulting from the dogged pursuit of more." They concluded, "We Americans have been pursuing more—more stuff, especially—for most of our history. We've been doing it to the exclusion of most other values since the 'me' decade of the 80s. . . . "[7] These authors describe the affluenza epidemic as an almost religious quest for economic expansion that has become the core principle for what is called "the American dream."[8]

The Malling of America

In 1986, Americans had more high schools than shopping centers. Less than fifteen years later, however, we had more than twice as many shopping centers as high schools. DeGraaf concluded, "Shopping centers have supplanted churches as a symbol of cultural values. In fact, seventy percent of us visit malls each week, more than attend houses of worship."[9]

Visiting the malls of America and covetously window shopping is materialism's equivalent of pornographic gazing for the sexual addict. In our consumer-driven culture, we're taught to never be satisfied—at least not for long. We become trapped in the cult of *the next thing.*[10] We are taught that our lives are measured by the abundance of our possessions and that the next thing we buy will finally be the item that brings us happiness.

We have become victims of the *Diderot Effect*.[11] The term arises from the eighteenth-century French philosopher, Denis Diderot (1713–1784), who, once upon a time, received a new, beautiful scarlet dressing gown. Having discarded his old gown, he began to conclude that his surroundings appeared shabby and unworthy of the grandeur exuded by his new garment. The pleasure of his garment turned sour as the splendor of the gown caused him eventually to replace his comfortable furnishings with newer and finer things, even if they lacked the well-worn features of his old stuff. He was dissatisfied with his study, with the threadbare tapestry, the desk, the chairs, and even the bookshelves. At the end of the day, Diderot found himself seated uncomfortably in the stylish formality of his new surroundings, regretting receiving his new scarlet robe that forced everything else around it to conform to its elegant tone.

The *Diderot Effect* keeps the consumer escalator moving ever upward. Like Diderot, we think we have to buy more and more, and enough is never enough. One hasty purchase leads to the next. Robert H. Frank, professor of economics at Cornell University, cited the futility of always buying more: "A host of careful studies suggest that across-the-board increases in our stocks of material goods produce virtually no measurable gains in our psychological or physical well-being."[12]

Consumerism claims that the material world is the only real world. Spiritual things are unimportant, and stuff brings us satisfaction. Paul, however, said we ought to look at what cannot be seen instead of what can be seen (2 Corinthians 4:18).

Consumerism also tells us that pleasure and power are found in the acquisition and consumption of material goods. We live in a world without limits, where anything seems possible and everything seems desirable. We have even convinced ourselves that the people who have accumulated the most material wealth are the most intelligent and diligent and, therefore, the most deserving of the goods they have acquired. The share of income going to the highest-earning one percent of Americans has doubled from eight percent in 1980 to more than sixteen percent in 2004.[13]

God and Gold

If Scripture is clear about anything, then riches and religion do not make very good partners. Jesus opposed our serving money when he declared, "No one can serve two masters, for either he will hate the one and love the other, or he will hold to one and despise the other. You cannot serve God and wealth. . . " (Matthew 6:24). Too, Jesus said, "How hard it is for those who are wealthy to enter the kingdom of God" (Luke 18:24b). Jesus told the rich young ruler, moreover, who inquired how he might find eternal life that he needed to sell his possessions and give the money to the poor. "He became very sad, for he was extremely rich" (Luke 18:23b; see Matt. 19:16–30; Mark 10:17–31). Jesus called on his followers not to "store up for yourselves treasures on earth, where moth and rust destroy, and where thieves break in and steal" (Matt. 6:19).

Paul concurred when he wrote, "But those who want to get rich fall into temptation and a snare and many foolish and harmful desires which plunge men into ruin and destruction. For the love of money is a root of all sorts of evil, and some by longing for it have wandered away from the faith, and pierced themselves with many griefs" (1 Timothy 6:9-10).

Giving Gold

A kingdom ethic of money reflects generosity, contentment, stewardship of creation, and servanthood. As a result, those who follow the Christian way should be generous in giving away their goods. Evidence shows, however, that the richer we become, the less we give in proportion to our incomes.[14]

In 1968, the average church member gave 3.1 percent of his or her income—a pitiful part of a tithe (10 percent). By 2003, that number had even dropped to 2.6 percent—only a quarter of the tithe.[15] John and Sylvia Ronsvalle have analyzed giving patterns of American Christians for more than thirty years. They pointed out that if American Christians had tithed in 2002, they would have had another $152 billion available to empower the poor and spread the gospel.[16] Putting this amount into perspective, current estimates are that about $80 billion a year would be enough to provide basic health care and education to all the poor of the earth.[17]

Several years ago, at a conference in New York City on social justice, a Native American stood up and said, "Regardless of what the New Testament says, most Christians are materialistic with no experience of the Spirit. . . . If you were Christians you would no longer accumulate. You would share everything you had."[18] Many Christians, indeed, practice an ethic of accumulation instead of one of sharing. Instead of tithing, we focus on giving ourselves greater gifts—bigger houses, better cars.

Tithing itself confronts at least partially our material addictions when practiced faithfully. Giving up ten percent of our income demands a fundamental change in our level of consumption. A middle-class couple who earns a combined household income of $80,000 would contribute a minimum of $8,000 to their local church. Giving such a gift would literally transform their lifestyle. They would probably drive less expensive cars or live in a more modest house because shifting $667 each month from selfish consumption to charitable giving would require a change in lifestyle.[19] Tithing empowers the church to do kingdom work and reminds the tither that God is the giver of all good gifts.

If we really follow Christ, how can we ignore Christ's church while we consume material goods in a manner identical to our unbelieving neighbors? How can the followers of a rabbi who had no place to lay his head (Matt. 8:20) live as crass consumers?

Like most problems, this one begins at the top. When prominent pastors and leaders in the Christian community live just like their secular counterparts, how can we expect the people in the pews to live any differently?

In the late 1970s, prominent evangelical leaders were attending a national conference. Several times in the group, there was a reference made to adopting a simple lifestyle. Finally, Loren Cunningham, the founder of Youth With A Mission, said something like this: "Yes, I think the evangelical community is ready to live more simply—if we evangelical leaders will model it." That ended the discussion. There were no further recommendations to live simply![20]

Upside Down

Jesus teaches his followers to see the world upside down: "So the last shall be first, and the first last" (Matt. 20:16). Those who follow Christ are not to judge others by the same standards by which society judges. Those who follow Christ are always to think about the underdog, the marginalized, and the downtrodden. The Old Testament prophets summarized sacred living as watching after widows and orphans (Isaiah 1:17; Jeremiah 7:6; 22:3; Zechariah 7:10; Malachi 3:5; see also James 1:27). In fact, in James we are told that the rich who had taken advantage of the minimum wage earners were going to find harsh punishment: "Behold, the pay of the laborers who mowed your fields, and which has been withheld by you, cries out against you . . ." (James 5:4). In the same epistle, James, the brother of Jesus, said that we should never show favoritism to the person who comes into church "with a gold ring and dressed in fine clothes" (James 2:2).

Christians tend to be partakers of the intoxicating power and prestige that accompanies wealth. In light of this, are Christians really willing to judge people based on something other than how much stuff they have accumulated or how much earning power they broker?

To affluent Americans, the poor have become invisible. We never drive on their side of town; we never look into their downcast eyes; and we pretend they do not exist. Many people work to make our lives easier—people we never acknowledge. There are busboys in restaurants and orderlies in the hospitals who live life on the ragged edge of poverty. Many of us seldom exchange a sentence with the host of workers who make our lives easier. Seemingly, we value them very little.

A story is told of a nursing student whose professor gave a pop quiz during the second month of school. She was a conscientious student and breezed through the questions until she read the last one: "What is the first name of the woman who cleans the school?" Surely this was some kind of joke. She had seen the cleaning woman several times. She was tall, dark-haired, and in her fifties, but how would a nursing student know her name? The student handed in her paper, leaving the last question blank. Before class ended, one student asked whether the last question would count toward the quiz grade. "Absolutely," said the professor. "In your careers, you will meet many people. All are significant. They deserve your attention and care, even if all you do is smile and say hello." The students never forgot that lesson. They also learned her name was Dorothy.

Jesus himself said the way we treat marginal members of society represents the way we treat him. In the great cosmic judgment scene in Matthew, Jesus says to those who are sent to eternal judgment:

> "I was hungry, and you gave Me nothing to eat; I was thirsty, and you gave Me nothing to drink; I was a stranger, and you did not invite Me in; naked, and you did not clothe Me; sick, and in prison, and you did not visit Me." Then they themselves also will answer, saying, "Lord, when did we see You hungry or thirsty, or a stranger, or naked, or sick, or in prison and did not take care of You?" Then He will answer them saying, "Truly I say to you, to the extent that you did not do it to one of the least of these, you did not do it to Me" (Matt. 25:42–45).

Wrecking Our Relationships

Not only should our approach to the material world be formulated by our following Jesus, but also the way we treat one another should be drastically changed by the fact that we are Jesus' disciples. We are to live by the Golden Rule—to treat others the same way we want them to treat us (Luke 6:31). We have to be honest, however, and ask ourselves the hard question: Do the commands of Christ really influence our relationships?

Marriage

No human relationship is more intimate than the relationship between a husband and a wife. This relationship, like no other, depicts the relationship between Christ and his church—Christ being the bridegroom and the church being the bride (Ephesians 5:22–33). Jesus is completely clear about his expectations for the permanency of the relationship between husbands and wives. He taught "that every one who divorces his wife, except for the reason of unchastity, makes her commit adultery. . ." (Matt. 5:32).

In contrast to Jesus, contemporary society asserts that divorce is the expected end to many marriages. Divorce has moved from the margins to the mainstream of American life over a thirty- to forty-year period. The core of the change, according to researcher Barbara Dafoe Whitehead, is a shift from a sense of obligation to family and society to an obligation to self. Once we began to focus on ourselves, rather than our families, divorce simply became part of an individual's pursuit for satisfaction, growth, and happiness. We have developed "the culture of divorce." Today, nearly half of all children are likely to experience parental divorce.[21]

Where do Christians fall in this self-centered search for happiness that ignores commitment to families and spouses? Shockingly, following Christ seemingly has no influence on our commitment to our spouse. Studies by the George Barna Research Group indicate that "born-again" Christians are as likely to go through a marital split as non-Christians! Thirty-five percent of "born-again" Christians are currently divorced or previously have been divorced. The figure is the same for people who do not consider themselves "born-again."[22] Christians seem simply to be reflecting the larger society's values and practices. How can the Lordship of Jesus have no impact on our most intimate of all relationships?

Human Sexuality

We are often wrecking our relationships in our approach to human sexuality. A growing pressure from our culture calls for couples to be sexually active outside of the covenant relationship of marriage. Society promotes, moreover, same-gender sexuality as "just another lifestyle." Those who refuse to bless same-gender relationships are often portrayed as full of bigotry.

Premarital Sex. More couples are living together outside of marriage than ever before, and the Bible belt has seen the greatest explosion of cohabitation. While national growth for the pattern of living together has averaged 72 percent during the 1990s, Oklahoma has seen a 97 percent increase, Tennessee a 123 percent increase, and Arkansas a 125 percent increase.[23] Barna also discovered that the cohabitation rate of "born-again" adults is only slightly lower than the general public.[24]

Once again, there is a great disparity between the purity we proclaim and the reality of our lifestyles as followers of Jesus. Shouldn't the Lordship of Jesus affect our lives more?

Same-Gender Sexuality. Mainline Protestant denominations often make the headlines of newspapers over the issue of same-gender sexuality.[25] Underneath the attention-grabbing headline, we find a story describing a segment within the denomination pushing for the acceptance of gay and lesbian lifestyles.

Once again, the church is merely reflecting society at large. The psychological community officially accepted same-gender sexuality as an alternative lifestyle when the American Psychiatric Association made the decision to delete homosexuality as a mental disorder from the Diagnostic and Statistical Manual in 1973.[26]

While I was serving in another congregation, I was ministering to a man who was dying of AIDS. It was well known that he had contracted AIDS through a homosexual lifestyle. I spent several months ministering to him during the period before his death. We talked about God's love, about sin, and about the forgiveness that is available through the cross of Christ Jesus.

After he died, I was invited to speak at his funeral. I knew it was going to be a very difficult task, to say the least. His father was an outstanding deacon; his mother was head of the Woman's Missionary Union. The man's family was a fine family in our church. The parents loved their son, and I had grown to love their son as well. The church was pondering, *Now, how is the pastor going to handle this one? What is he going to say at the funeral? Is he going to pretend that the elephant is not in the room and just deliver accolade upon accolade for the son who has passed away?* I also knew that another group would measure every word—the gay community from a larger city where he had actively practiced a homosexual lifestyle. I knew they would want to hear something quite different from what the family and church expected to hear.

At the funeral, I talked about what an outstanding person their son was—positive things could easily be said about this young man. But at a pivotal point in the message I delivered these words.

> *John Doe was a sinner. You can be sure of that. I am a sinner. You can be even more sure of that. But as all sinners, John Doe did not come to his God, his church, or his family seeking acceptance. Acceptance could not and would not be given. Rather, John came to God, came to his church, and came to his family seeking forgiveness. And that, on all accounts, has already been granted.*

The family was pleased because I had treated their son with respect, as I treat all of us who are sinners and have been given God's grace. About a week passed, however, and I received this anonymous letter in the mail.

> *Dear Pastor,*
>
> *John Doe was our friend. He was a very sweet person who died a very tragic death. The reason we're writing this letter is because we can't get out of our minds a number of things that were said at his funeral. They have hurt and angered us. The God we know and love is very kind and gentle, who loves all people equally. We find ourselves bewildered that in a church service full of people who are suffering the loss of a loved one, such anger and disrespect and condemnation would be shown under the guise of easing the suffering of this terrible loss. To say that John did not ask acceptance and would not have been given acceptance, either by God or by the congregation, but that he was forgiven is neither comforting to those of us who have lost a loved one, but, even more so, not the doctrine that the God we worship has shown us. Our God teaches love above all things and is not accepting of the judgment of one group of people by another group of people. It was shocking*

to hear those words, especially from a church leader, especially at a time like this. It must take a lot of energy to be so full of bigotry that you would stand over a young man at his funeral and choose words such as these that would insult the life that he lived here on earth. Our God is much more accepting than this. We pray that you and the people who follow you will try to be more loving and accepting and less judgmental and hurtful.

I read the letter more than once, of course. The more I thought about the letter, though, the more I came to the conclusion that I would not have changed a single word in the funeral service. While I had withstood the pressure to accept his lifestyle, I felt confident that I had lovingly included him within the circle of God's grace. Despite my best efforts, however, the gay community found offensive my refusal to completely condone homosexuality.

The church is going to face a growing pressure to accept same-gender sexuality or be accused of narrow-minded bigotry. Homosexuality is going to be a watershed issue in church life in the coming years.

Baptists cannot safely sit on the sideline and watch other denominations struggle with same-gender sexuality. If we are going to follow Christ, if we are going to follow the teachings of his earliest and closest followers, the apostles, we must go to Scripture as the supreme authority for our decisions.

I am well aware that there are competing ideas in genetics, biology, and psychology about the issue of same-gender sexuality. In the final analysis, however, it is not contemporary science that should decide how the church will respond to the issue. In fact, what is good science today may well be relegated to the footnotes of the next generation's textbook. And what is considered good psychological theory today may well be considered poor practice by the next generation of therapists.

In Romans 1, Paul searched for a sin that represented perversity and illustrated that all creation had gone awry. He alluded to the Genesis account in which humanity was created—male and female—in the image of God and told to be fruitful and multiply. Man was told to leave his father and his mother, and woman was told to leave her home. They were to cleave to each other and become one flesh (Genesis 1:27–28; 2:24). In Romans 1, Paul gives heterosexuality nothing less than the theological grounding of creation itself.

Every biblical passage that addresses the issue of same-gender sexuality casts it in a negative light. There is not a single exception. The potential discovery of biological or psychological foundations for same-gender sexuality does not mean it should be accepted by the church. There are many behaviors that are not acceptable in the community of Christ that might have a biological predisposition. Alcoholism, for example, is believed to have a biological basis, but drunkenness is not acceptable. Even gambling, some would claim, has a physiological basis.[27] Many destructive behaviors can be traced to our biological or psychological heritage. In fact, each one of us has a predisposition to be greedy, lustful, and covetous.

Being Christian means that we struggle against our inherent desires of the flesh (Galatians 5:13–25). We flee from the faults of the flesh and try to walk a more noble path as Christ calls us to come and follow him.

As the people of God, we cannot baptize sin and make it acceptable. To do so is to be less than authentic with those who are struggling with any particular sin. To tell someone same-gender sexuality is acceptable when God's word says that it is strictly forbidden is morally wrong for the pastor, counselor, or church.

The church should never change the definition of sin to please popular culture. Denominations should not struggle with the issue of same-gender sexuality when it is clearly forbidden in God's word. If we call Jesus *Lord*, we cannot label any sin as acceptable. The prophetic voice of God's people should not be muted in order to conform to culture.

Discrimination

What Martin Luther King, Jr. observed decades ago is still true today: no hour is more segregated in America than eleven o'clock on Sunday morning.[28] We have chosen to separate ourselves from people who are different from us at the time we gather as God's children to praise him.

While the civil rights reformer was making reference to racial segregation, other types of segregation have become just as pronounced. Churches spring up every day that seek to reach only narrow parameters of people.[29]

Churches, for example, might be formed in order to reach college students in a university town or artists or singles in metropolitan areas. More than ever before, churches are being formed for the stated purpose of reaching one age group, one felt-needs group, or one segment of an ethnic group.

While these churches may reach people that traditional churches may never reach, they need to consider the larger ramifications of such a strategy. They need to seek to be intentionally diverse in every possible way. When we worship only with people like us, we rob ourselves of the multi-cultural, multi-generational experience that early believers eventually learned to embrace as recorded in the Acts of the Apostles. Traditional churches who claim to include everyone, moreover, must ask themselves the hard question: *How could we change ourselves to form a more diverse congregation, to reach all people?*

In a culture that contains many races, why are the great majority of churches limited to a single ethnic group? What are the followers of Christ communicating to the world when we are more segregated than society? Secular schools have been integrated, but many churches remain attended by only one race. Thus, we have communicated that secular society is stronger than anything faith can produce.

Sociologist George Yancey asserted that Christians undermine their ability to reach society with the gospel because they segregate their churches by race. According to Yancey, only eight percent of churches are multi-racial—defined as a church in which no single racial group comprises more than eighty percent of the participants.[30]

The church-growth movement has long promoted the *homogeneous unit principle* for growing churches. Put plainly, this principle teaches that churches "of one kind of people only are more effective in winning others of the same people."[31] Church growth strategist Peter Wagner went so far as to say, "Mixing peoples has often proved to be another wrong method."[32] Such well-intentioned, but simplistic, strategies for church growth were strongly promoted in seminaries during the late twentieth century. Unfortunately, this push for *people like me* churches was often embraced without question, and many denominations seeking growth neglected diversity.

Multi-racial churches are important because the community of Christ ought to be leading in racial reconciliation rather than lagging behind. Following Christ means breaking barriers.

Clarence Jordan was a Baptist New Testament scholar who founded a multi-racial community, Koinonia Farm, in the segregated Deep South in 1942. He wrote, "For three years [Jesus] taught by parable, precept, and practice the Father's love for the people of the whole world."[33]

The ministry of Jesus is highlighted by the fact that he was kind to Samaritans, the most despised people group to the average Jew. Jesus traveled through Samaria and spoke to the woman at the well to show he was Savior of the whole world (John 4). Even she was shocked. She was so shocked that she asked, "How is it that You, *being a Jew*, ask me for a drink since I am a *Samaritan woman?*" (John 4:9b, italics added for emphasis). In the story of the ten cleansed lepers, only the Samaritan leper returned to give thanks to Jesus (Luke 17:12–19). In fact, one of Jesus' most loved parables has garnered the title "The Good Samaritan" (Luke 10:30–37). Jesus spoke fondly of Samaritans to Jews in order that the Jews would see that God's love transcends all barriers, races, and people groups. If we are going to call Jesus *Lord*, we must be color blind. No gathering should be more accepting of all races than Sunday morning worship.

One church in Arkansas defies racial barriers as well as social barriers. Among the 400 in attendance, you will find a United States Senator, a former professional basketball star, a local television anchor woman, an alcoholic, a Middle Eastern convert from Islam, a disabled teenager, an attorney, and an illegal immigrant. The leadership is deliberately multi-ethnic, including people from African-American, Puerto Rican, and Chinese descent. One in five of the church's attendees is Latino, and many don't speak English. The worship style changes from week to week in order to appeal to the diverse groups in the congregation. While the pastor admits the various groups do not enjoy the worship styles equally, they esteem unity over style.[34]

Churches must also embrace the elderly. In a culture that worships youthfulness, churches have often been guilty of quickly pushing senior adults aside. Such churches might relegate them to an early, traditional worship service so that the desires of younger worshipers can dominate a separate, more highly attended service. When young families flee to a separate service designed just for them, many senior adults are robbed of their only weekly contact with children. This isolation comes from the fact that their own grandchildren might live four states away.[35] The biblical church, however, was multigenerational (Acts 2:44). In Titus, Paul instructed older women to serve as mentors for younger women (Titus 2:3–5). The church, of all institutions, should be showing honor to the aged. While offering multiple styles of worship in separate services might be the most effective way for some congregations to reach more people, churches should make every effort to find creative ways to foster interaction between all generations of members.

Walking in the Spirit

Those who call Jesus *Lord* are indwelt by the Holy Spirit of God. We cannot resist temptation by our own strength. Walking by the Spirit, however, we "will not carry out the desires of the flesh" (Galatians 5:17). A war wages within between the flesh and the Spirit. As we yield ourselves to the Spirit, our lives are not dominated by fleshly desires. On the contrary, we show evidence of the fruit of the Spirit in our lives: "love, joy, peace, patience, kindness, goodness, faithfulness, gentleness, self-control" (Gal. 5:22–23). Paul concluded, "Those who belong to Christ Jesus have crucified the flesh with its passions and desires. If we live by the Spirit, let us also walk by the Spirit" (Gal. 5:24–25).

Conclusion

If we are going to call Jesus *Lord*, then we must demonstrate Jesus' Lordship in our daily lives. Jesus said, "Not every one who says to Me, 'Lord, Lord,' will enter the kingdom of heaven, but he who does the will of My Father. . . " (Matt. 7:21).

In every arena, from our handling of material goods to our treatment of people, we must show evidence of Jesus' rule in our lives. The church damages the image of Christ when we trample over Christ's commands and ignore Christ's example of obedience. To call Jesus *Lord* is to live Jesus' way.

CHAPTER *Seven*
Jesus—King of the Cosmos

To call Jesus Lord *means Jesus is King of the cosmos.*

A GIRL WAS RETURNING FROM SUNDAY School and sat by a man on the city bus. The man, apparently a skeptic, observed her Sunday School literature and decided to make fun of her faith. He challenged, "If you can tell me where God is, I'll give you an apple." Without hesitation, the girl replied, "Sir, if you can tell me a place where God is not, I'll give you a *basket* of apples."

When applied to the Lordship of Jesus, the truth is stated this way: *There is no place where Jesus is not Lord.* When we acknowledge the Lordship of Jesus, we are declaring Jesus' supreme authority over every realm. He is King of the entire cosmos. The Lordship of the resurrected Christ has no limits, no boundaries, and no restrictions. As Jesus sits enthroned at the right hand of God, no being in the physical or spiritual world has supremacy over the exalted Lord Jesus. From every perspective, Jesus' rule is limitless, for Jesus is ruler over Jews and Gentiles, believers and unbelievers, the living and the dead, the present world and the world to come, and all spiritual forces and authorities.

Lord over Jews and Gentiles

Peter, the spokesman for the twelve disciples, preached his first sermon in the Acts of the Apostles on the Jewish Day of Pentecost—a harvest festival. Following the outpouring of God's Spirit, Peter raised his voice and preached to "Men of *Judea* and all you who live in *Jerusalem*" (Acts 2:14, italics added for emphasis). Pulling passages from the prophets and the Psalms, Peter explained the outpouring of God's Spirit as evidence of God's sovereign hand in all that had happened to Jesus—"This Man, delivered over by the predetermined plan and foreknowledge of God" (Acts 2:23a). Although they had nailed Jesus to the cross (Acts 2:23b), God raised him from the power of death (2:24) and placed him in the position of authority at God's own right hand (2:33).[1]

Having connected the story of Jesus to both the prophets and the psalmist (David), Peter brought his Pentecost sermon to a climax when he concluded, "Therefore let all the *house of Israel* know for certain that God has made Him both *Lord* and Christ. . . " (2:36, italics added for emphasis). With this statement, Peter wed the crucified, Jewish Messiah (the Christ) with the resurrected Lord of the cosmos. The glory of the enthroned Lord stands sovereign, in sharp contrast to the Jesus whom they had crucified. At this festival gathering in Jerusalem, Jews who had traveled "from every nation under heaven" (2:5) heard the Lordship of the Messiah proclaimed.[2]

In another sermon Peter preached, we learn that Gentiles are also included under the Lordship of Christ. This was a lesson the apostle himself had to learn. Having been divinely prepared by a visionary experience (Acts 10:9–16),[3] Peter declared to the household of Cornelius, his Gentile audience, "I most certainly understand now that God is not one to show partiality, but in *every nation* the man who fears Him and does what is right, is welcome to Him" (Acts 10:34b–35, italics added for emphasis). Asserting that God is God of the Gentile as well as the Jew, Peter made a prophetic declaration that summarized his sermon: "He is *Lord of all*" (Acts 10:36b, italics added for emphasis).[4] Before Peter's very eyes, the Holy Spirit fell on the Gentile believers. They received the Spirit of God, just as the Jewish converts had received the Spirit of God (Acts 10:44). He reported to the council at Jerusalem: "We believe that we [Jews] are saved through the grace of the *Lord* Jesus, in the same way as they [Gentiles] also are" (Acts 15:11, italics added for emphasis).

Like Peter, Paul saw the Lordship of Jesus transcending the barrier between Jews and Gentiles. In his letter to Christians in Rome, Paul concluded, " . . . There is no distinction between Jew and Greek; for the same Lord is lord of all, abounding in riches for all who call on Him, for WHOEVER WILL CALL ON THE NAME OF THE LORD WILL BE SAVED" (Romans 10:12–13; see also Acts 20:21; Rom. 1:16; Galatians 3:28). Therefore, both Jew and Greek receive salvation the same way—through confessing the Lordship of Jesus.

Lord over Believers and Unbelievers

Being a believer means yielding to Christ's Lordship (1 Corinthians 1:2; 2 Corinthians 4:5; 2 Timothy 2:22). Those who had committed themselves to following Jesus found it natural to refer to him as "*our Lord* Jesus Christ." In the letter from the Jerusalem Council in Acts 15, we find Barnabas and Paul described as: ". . . men who have risked their lives for the name of *our Lord* Jesus Christ" (Acts 15:26, italics added for emphasis). When Paul was giving his farewell speech to the elders of Ephesus, moreover, he summarized his ministry among them as ". . . solemnly testifying to both Jews and Greeks of repentance toward God and faith in *our Lord* Jesus Christ" (Acts 20:21, italics added for emphasis). The early believers declared Jesus as their Lord without hesitation.

Make no mistake about it. Although one may refuse the rule and realm of Christ in this world, ultimately Jesus is Lord of all—both of those who choose to believe and those who refuse to believe. Part of Jesus' Lordship over believers and unbelievers alike includes placing judgment on them. The way that one responds to Jesus determines that individual's eternal reward or punishment (Matthew 10:32–33; Mark 8:38). The announcement, "The kingdom of God has come near" (Luke 10:9, 11), becomes a threat rather than a promise for those who refuse to accept the message. For the unbeliever, Jesus' Lordship does not bring salvation but damnation (Matt. 23:33). Jesus himself said not everyone who calls him "Lord, Lord" will have the opportunity to enter into the kingdom of heaven. Rather, it is the one "who does the will of My Father who is in heaven" (Matt. 7:21).[5] For Jesus will declare to the one who acknowledges his Lordship in word only, "DEPART FROM ME, YOU WHO PRACTICE LAWLESSNESS" (Matt. 7:23).

When Jesus returns, both believers and unbelievers will see and acknowledge Jesus' Lordship, for, at that point: "EVERY KNEE WILL BOW . . . and . . . every tongue will confess that Jesus Christ is Lord, to the glory of God the Father" (Philippians 2:10-11). Although unbelievers may not yield to Jesus' sovereignty now, they eventually will have no choice but to pay homage to Jesus. The return of the Lord Jesus Christ is the definitive event that places both believers and unbelievers under Jesus' Lordship. For the one it ensures salvation, and for the other it ensures separation from God (1 Thessalonians 5:3; 2 Thessalonians 1:7-9; Revelation 20:11-15).

Paul's most developed thoughts on judgment are found in Romans 2. On the day of judgment (Rom. 2:5), God will judge all people through Christ Jesus according to their works (2:6).[6] While those who are believers receive eternal life, the wicked receive the wrath of God (2:6-10).

Paul elsewhere made it clear that all people must stand before the judgment seat of Christ (2 Cor. 5:10), which is the same as the judgment seat of God (Rom. 14:10). Because of their belief in Christ, however, those who follow him need not be afraid (Rom. 8:33-34). Even believers, nonetheless, will be judged according to their works. Although a believer's salvation is secure, judgment will examine how he or she has built on the foundation of faith in Christ Jesus (1 Cor. 3:12-15).[7]

Lord over the Living and the Dead

Because Jesus' Lordship knows no boundaries, even death itself does not release us from the authority of the resurrected Christ. Paul wrote, "For not one of us lives for himself, and not one of us dies for himself; for if we live, we live for the Lord, or if we die, we die for the Lord; therefore, whether we live or die, we are the Lord's. For to this end Christ died and lived again, that He might be *Lord both of the dead and the living*" (Rom. 14:7–9, italics added for emphasis).

In the Christological hymn found in Philippians 2:6–11, moreover, Paul asserted that although Christ had become a bond servant who humbled himself in death, ultimately "those who are in heaven and on the earth and under the earth" (Phil. 2:10) would acknowledge his Lordship. With this comprehensive statement, Paul was saying that both the living and dead would be required to acknowledge openly the Lord's authority over them. In 2 Timothy, Paul described Christ Jesus as the one "who is to judge the *living and the dead*. . . " (2 Tim. 4:1, italics added for emphasis). All of us, therefore, will give an account of ourselves to God. Even the boundary of death does not exclude one from the authority of Christ.

Lord over This World and the World to Come

Although we currently live in "this present evil age" (Gal. 1:4), and Satan can be described as "the god of this world" (2 Cor. 4:4), Jesus is Lord over this world. When Jesus arrived, the kingdom of God arrived, although Jesus' Lordship was present at that time in something of a secret way. Appearing among humanity as a human being, his role was that of a suffering servant rather than the glorified Lord.[8] As New Testament theologian George Ladd described the siutation, "The future, heavenly Son of Man is already present among men but in a form they hardly expected."[9] Jesus' present rule found its hinge point at his enthronement as he now sits at the very right hand of God (Ephesians 1:20–23; Philippians 2:9). Therefore, we must think of Christ as already having begun his kingly reign at his ascension. The New Testament portrays Christ reigning from his heavenly throne (Acts 2:33–36; Hebrews 1:3, 13; 8:1; 10:12–13; 12:2).[10] Jesus is already King (1 Cor. 15:24–26; Rev. 3:21).

While Jesus' reign has already begun in a real sense, his reign is unseen and unrecognized by the world. Jesus' glory is now known only to people of faith. The day is coming, though, when Jesus' glory will be made known to all, and every enemy will be put under his feet (1 Cor. 15:25). This climactic reign will come in public power and glory. Jesus' Lordship will at last be recognized universally (Phil. 2:10–11; Rev. 19:11–21).[11]

In the New Testament, Christians longing for the full and glorious reign of Christ declared, "Maranatha" (1 Cor. 16:22). The term *marana tha* is Aramaic and is most often understood to mean *our Lord, come.*[12] Taking Revelation 22:20 and 1 Corinthians 16:22 together, *marana tha* is best interpreted as a prayer seeking the victorious return of Christ. Ironically, in a letter written to a Greek-speaking church like Corinth, the Aramaic term *marana tha* was left untranslated. The best explanation for this curiosity is clear. *Marana tha* quickly became a familiar expression even among the Gentiles as Christians longed for Jesus' fully present Lordship in the world to come.[13]

Jesus himself declared his Second Coming when the high priest questioned him. When Jesus was on trial, the high priest asked him whether he was the Messiah, the Son of God. Jesus answered, "I am" (Mark 14:62), and continued, "You shall see THE SON OF MAN SITTING AT THE RIGHT HAND OF POWER, and COMING WITH THE CLOUDS OF HEAVEN" (Mark 14:62).[14] Jesus, therefore, is Lord of both this world—even if his Lordship is not yet fully recognized—and the world to come.

Lord over All Spiritual Forces and Authorities

The cosmic war between the kingdom of God and the evil of this age is depicted in Scripture in various ways. One way Scripture depicts this cosmic war is as a struggle between light and darkness. Being born in Bethlehem as the only Son of God (John 3:16), Christ arrived as light in the midst of darkness. Darkness has made every effort to overcome the light, but to no avail: "The light shines in the darkness, and the darkness did not comprehend it" (John 1:5). We should have no question about the identity of the light, for Jesus declared, "I am the Light of the world; he who follows Me will not walk in the darkness, but will have the Light of life" (John 8:12). Those who believe in the light become sons of the light (John 12:36).

Even though the light has arrived, people find themselves still loving darkness rather than light. Because of their evil deeds, they refuse to walk in the light (John 3:19). In fact, those who do evil are accused of actually hating the light because they do not want their deeds exposed. Those who walk in the truth, however, come into the light unashamed of their deeds (John 3:21).

Despite making every attempt to thwart the purposes of God concerning humanity's redemption, the kingdom of darkness has not been able to halt the will and the way of God. As we examine the New Testament, we discover that Jesus is Lord over all spiritual forces and authorities, including Satan, his demonic forces, and cosmic powers.

Satan

The primary purpose of Satan is to interrupt and thwart God's plan of salvation for creation, especially humanity. At the very onset of his ministry, Jesus was led into the wilderness to be tempted by the devil himself (Matt. 4:1). Satan sought to lure the Lord to choose instant glory over obedience to God. Showing Jesus all the kingdoms of the world, the devil said to Jesus, "I will give You all this domain and its glory; for it has been handed over to me, and I give it to whomever I wish" (Luke 4:6).

Trying to halt God's redemptive purposes, Satan offered the Son of God glory without suffering, thus attempting to thwart God's plan for redemption. The tempter knew well that by suffering and dying on the cross, Jesus would satisfy God's wrath against humanity's sin. He knew that those who submitted themselves to the crucified Christ would be free from the bondage of sin and death should the plan of redemption proceed. Therefore, the devil offered Jesus a *cross-less* path of messiahship.[15]

Later in Jesus' ministry, Jesus depicted himself as being powerful enough to bind Satan, the "strong man" (Matt. 12:28–29). Having bound the enemy, Jesus said he was plundering "the strong man's house"—that is, casting out demons (12:28–29).[16] As part of Jesus' conflict with Satan, Jesus also sought to curb the power of the evil one through his disciples' acts of exorcism. Jesus found joy in the fact that the demons were being defeated when his disciples used the authority of his name. Seeing his disciples' command over demons, Jesus replied, "I was watching Satan fall from heaven like lightning" (Luke 10:18). Through Christ, God has invaded human history and begun the triumph over evil.

Although Jesus himself predicted Satan's fall with the statement just quoted from Luke 10:18, the ultimate victory is not accomplished until the end of the age.[17] While somewhat restrained, Satan is, nonetheless, busy trying to snatch away the word of the kingdom from hearts too hard to receive it (Mark 4:15). He even spoke through the Apostle Peter, urging Jesus to take a different road from the road that led to redemption through the cross (Mark 8:32).[18] At Peter's attempt to divert the Messiah's suffering, Jesus declared, "Get behind Me, *Satan*" (Mark 8:33, italics added for emphasis).

The Book of Revelation depicts the final scenes of the great conflict between good and evil. Following a period of terrible evil in human history in which the powers of evil wage war against the church and seek to exercise worldwide rule (Rev. 13:1–10), God ultimately defeats the devil. Satan himself seeks to destroy the Messiah (Rev. 12:4–5), but finds himself cast down from his place of power (12:10–12; 20:10). The Lamb is ultimately victorious because he is "Lord of lords and King of kings" (17:14; see 19:16).

Demons

Jesus' having power over the prince of demons, Satan, also meant having power over Satan's demonic forces (Mark 3:22–27). As we summarize the ministry of Jesus from the synoptic Gospels (Matthew, Mark, and Luke), we see there are three major elements: Jesus taught; Jesus healed; and Jesus cast out demons.[19] Because of Jesus' authority over the demonic forces, the crowd responded with amazement: "What is this? A new teaching with authority! He commands even the unclean spirits, and they obey Him" (Mark 1:27).

The heart of the Messiah's mission was to overcome the evil that encumbers humanity. People's souls are battlegrounds, and Jesus came to release them from bondage to demonic powers. By casting out demons, Jesus was declaring that the kingdom of God had arrived and ultimate victory was secure (Matt. 12:28).

Cosmic Powers

Alongside Satan and demons, the New Testament describes superhuman forces as "principalities and powers."[20] As a result of extensive development of this concept in Judaism, principalities and powers came to represent divisions of angelic beings (not necessarily good) and powers in the sphere above the earth (see Daniel 7:27).[21] For example, in both Romans 8:38 and 1 Peter 3:22, principalities and powers are clearly associated with angelic beings. The New Testament writers speculate little about these powers but often connect them to Christ's work.[22]

These created angelic beings (Colossians 1:16) are subject to Christ through his death, resurrection, and enthronement: "[Jesus Christ] is at the right hand of God, having gone into heaven, after angels and authorities and powers had been subjected to Him" (1 Pet. 3:22). Christ sits enthroned above every rule and authority and power and dominion (Eph. 1:20-21) and is the head of every rule and authority (Col. 2:10) for the sake of his people, the church (Eph. 1:22).

These forces seem to participate in some negative aspects of the created world (Eph. 6:12). They are part of God's creation, but they have fallen. Despite our difficulty in understanding these forces, one thing is clear: they are subject to the Lordship of Jesus.[23]

Death

As the resurrected Christ is placing all enemies under his feet, the last enemy to be defeated is death itself: "Then comes the end, when He hands over the kingdom to the God and Father, when He has abolished all rule and all authority and power. For He must reign until He has put all His enemies under His feet. The last enemy that will be abolished is death" (1 Cor. 15:24–26).

Because Jesus took on human form and yet defeated death (Heb. 2:14–15), all of humankind has been empowered to pass from "death into life" (John 5:24) by believing in him (5:24–25; 11:25–26). Jesus' death becomes our death and Jesus' resurrection our resurrection (Rom. 6:3–5; compare 2 Cor. 4:10–11). In Christ, death has lost its sting (1 Cor. 15:55).

Glory to God

Jesus claimed to be the presence of God. He was the very glory of God dwelling among his people.[24] While there is no limit to Jesus' Lordship when the age to come finally arrives, Jesus is not seeking to glorify himself. He glorifies the Father. When Jesus has subdued every hostile enemy, he will turn the kingdom over to God the Father that God may be "utterly supreme over everything everywhere" (1 Cor. 15:28, New Living Translation).[25] The purpose of acknowledging the Son's Lordship is so he can give glory to the Father: ". . . every tongue will confess that Jesus Christ is Lord, to the glory of God the Father" (Phil. 2:11).

Conclusion

To say "Jesus is Lord" is to say Jesus is King of the cosmos. Jesus' rule and reign have no limit.

All people (both Jews and Gentiles), whether living or dead, are under Jesus' authority. Even rejecting Jesus does not remove one from Jesus' power as Lord. Ultimately, there is no way to deny the authority and power of the resurrected and enthroned Lord.

Conclusion

This Book's and Yours

T WO THOUSAND YEARS HAVE PASSED, and the followers of Jesus still call him *Lord*. You cannot sincerely call Jesus *Lord* unless you belong to him, and you cannot belong to Jesus unless you call him *Lord*.

What did Jesus' earliest followers mean when they declared, "Jesus is Lord"? Take a brief review of what we've learned in this study. Along the way, consider carefully what saying "Jesus is Lord" means to you.

The Heart of the Christian Faith

Only one idea—the Lordship of Jesus—serves as the heart of all that is held true by Christians (see chapter 1). We must comprehend what it means to call Jesus *Lord* if we are ever to grasp the message of the New Testament.

Jesus Is God

How could the birth of a poor Jewish infant mean so much (see chapter 2)? The baby grew to be a carpenter and rabbi from the little hamlet known as Nazareth. While the other rabbis talked about God as if God were far away, Jesus claimed to be one with the Father (see John 10:38). Jesus' radical claim, which placed Jesus on par with God, elicited cries of blasphemy from the Jews who opposed him. They were ready to stone him. In calling Jesus *Lord*, however, we are affirming Jesus' statement about himself when he said, "I am in the Father, and the Father is in Me" (John 14:11).

The writers of the New Testament present Jesus as having the power of God the Father in many ways. Consider just three examples: (1) Jesus had the power to forgive sins (see Mark 2:7); (2) Jesus was superior to the Sabbath (2:28); and (3) Jesus defeated the demons, who fearfully declared his divinity (1:24). The earliest Christians concluded that they were under the obligation to worship Jesus, even as they worshiped God, because they saw the Father and the Son as one.

The Kingdom Has Come

Given the many ways Jesus possessed the power of God and was the presence of God, to call Jesus *Lord* was to declare that the day of the Lord had finally arrived and the kingdom of God was present (see chapter 3). The ancient Israelites had been waiting for the great *day of the Lord* when God would intervene on their behalf, overturning injustice, righting all wrongs, and freeing them from the oppression of foreign rule.[1] The day of the Lord was an event whereby God intervened on behalf of ancient Israel by judging the pagan nations. Humanity's rebellion would come to a close, and the period of God's sovereignty would begin (see Joel 2; Isaiah 13–14). The day of the Lord was the pivotal hinge that connected human history with the eternal kingdom of God.

Surprising his contemporaries, Jesus proclaimed that the kingdom of God had already arrived with his very presence. The summary of Jesus' preaching, as presented by the Gospel writers, is certain and succinct: "Repent, for the kingdom of heaven *is at hand*" (Matthew 4:17, italics added for emphasis). When the Pharisees questioned Jesus about "when the kingdom of God was coming" (Luke 17:20), Jesus replied, "The kingdom of God is not coming with signs to be observed; nor will they say, 'Look, here it is!' or 'There it is!' For behold, the kingdom of God is in your midst" (Luke 17:21).

Death Is Defeated

Because Jesus' Lordship demands his resurrection, New Testament scholar N. T. Wright correctly concluded that while ingenious scholars have invented forms of Christianity that do not hold to the resurrection of Jesus, early Christianity without exception affirmed Jesus' resurrection.[2] The resurrection of Jesus is central to New Testament Christianity.[3]

To say "Jesus is Lord," therefore, is to believe that God has powerfully raised Jesus from the dead, even if we do not understand how this could be (see chapter 4). To acknowledge the Lordship of Jesus is to see him in an exalted light and to have faith in the risen Christ.[4]

A New Family Is Formed

Our culture promotes individual spirituality. Thus, many people claim to be followers of Jesus, and yet they never gather with Jesus' people to worship on Sunday, Jesus' resurrection day. When we call Jesus *Lord*, we find our place in the family of those who worship him (see chapter 5).

In the New Testament, Christians are depicted as loving one another as close family, as loving brothers and sisters love one another.[5] Using language that commonly described the love shared in a biological family, the New Testament portrays the love experienced among God's people: "Now as to the *love of the brethren*, you have no need for anyone to write to you, for you yourselves are taught by God to love one another" (1 Thessalonians 4:9, italics added for emphasis). The idea of believers sharing the love of a family is commonplace in the New Testament (Romans 12:10; Hebrews 13:1; 1 Peter 1:22; 2 Peter 1:7).

Following the New Testament admonition to see one another as loving siblings, John concluded that we cannot love God, whom we *have not* seen, if we do not love our brother, whom we *have* seen. Loving one's fellow Christians is an essential element of loving God (1 John 4:20–21). This family-like love among God's people finds biblical expression in a local church.

Live Jesus' Way

When we call Jesus *Lord*, we commit ourselves to following the path of the sinless Savior (see chapter 6). We submit our fleshly desires to Jesus' kingdom values. While we find forgiveness in Jesus' Lordship, Christianity is no license to sin freely. Paul wrote, "Are we to continue in sin so that grace might increase? May it never be! How shall we who died to sin still live in it?" (Rom. 6:1b–2). We are not to take God's grace for granted.

In reality, however, we often fail to follow Jesus' example of obedience. Sometimes Christians seem to walk just as the world walks, don't they?

If, though, we are going to call Jesus *Lord*, then we must show the evidence of Jesus' Lordship in our daily lives. Jesus said, "Not every one who says to Me, 'Lord, Lord,' will enter the kingdom of heaven, but he who does the will of My Father..." (Matt. 7:21). In every arena, from how we deal with materialistic temptations to how we treat people, we must show evidence of Jesus' rule in our lives. The church damages the image of Jesus when we trample over Jesus' commands and ignore Jesus' example of obedience. To call Jesus *Lord* is to live like Jesus.

A King Is Crowned

There is no place and no power that escapes the rule and reign of Jesus (see chapter 7). When we acknowledge the Lordship of Jesus, we are declaring Jesus' supreme authority over every realm. He is King of the entire cosmos. The Lordship of the resurrected Jesus has no limits, no boundaries, and no restrictions. As Jesus sits enthroned at the right hand of God, no being in the physical or spiritual world has supremacy over the exalted Lord Jesus. From every perspective, Jesus' rule is limitless, for Jesus is ruler over Jews and Gentiles, believers and unbelievers, the living and the dead, the present world and the world to come, and all spiritual forces and authorities.

A Decision Determines

So, how will you respond? The crucified and resurrected Christ claimed to be the very Son of God who ushered in God's kingdom. You must determine whether you will yield your life to Jesus' Lordship.

Several years ago, a prominent businessperson made a visit to my office. His soul-wrenching search had been preceded over the years by many other visitors to my office and would be repeated by many to follow. As had others before him, he asked questions like these: *Where do I find the meaning of life? Who was Jesus? How can I put the pieces of my broken life back together? How do I mend my miserable marriage?* All these questions are simply versions of the same larger question: *How do I find the Lord of the cosmos, and how am I to follow him?*

I responded to the man's search with a story about a Jewish rabbi who was obedient in following his Father's commands all the way to a horrible death on the cross. Death, however, was powerless over this Christ of the cosmos, the sinless Savior of humanity. He victoriously emerged from the grave that sought to hold him captive. This crucified and resurrected Lord invites all to yield their story to his story, to follow him after they have carefully counted the cost. The call is to give allegiance to Jesus' Lordship and to follow Jesus in obedience.

The businessman looked terribly burdened as he began to understand the call of the Christ—the call to live under Jesus' Lordship. He left pondering a decision that would determine his eternal destiny. I could not make the decision for him and did little more than lay out the message of the Lordship of Jesus. I prayed for him, but his decision of discipleship belonged to him alone. I wondered: *Will he ever yield his will to the way of God?*

Years later I ran into him at a community-wide Christian event. "I followed him," he said with a smile of relief. I could tell the war within him was over. The forces that were seeking to destroy his life and his family were powerless, for he had joined forces with the resurrected Lord. He excitedly told me about his healed marriage and his hope-filled future. These results came when he surrendered control of his life to the Lord Jesus Christ. He was actively pursuing his discipleship in a local church with which he was identified at that community-wide Christian event, and he had joined his entire family to God's family.

I know how *his* story ends, but only you can write the words that will alter *your* life forever. Will you seek the Son of God as your Savior or permit the god of self or the powers of sin and death to continue to rule over you?

To refuse Jesus' Lordship is to fall into the fool's folly. To call Jesus *Lord* is to dedicate your whole being to Jesus as you crown him King of the cosmos and King of your life. To call Jesus *Lord* is to say everything.

Notes

About This Doctrine, Heritage, and Life Study

1. Previous resources produced for this series include the following: *Back to Bedrock* by Paul W. Powell; *Back to Bedrock Teaching Guide* by Dennis Parrot; *The Bible—You Can Believe It* by James C. Denison; and *The Bible—You Can Believe It: Teaching Guide* by Larry Shotwell. See the order form at the end of this book.

Introduction

1. Unless otherwise indicated, all Scripture quotations in this book are from the New American Standard Bible® (1995 edition).

Chapter One

1. Robert H. Mounce, *The Essential Nature of New Testament Preaching* (Grand Rapids: Eerdmans, 1960), 94.

2. George Eldon Ladd, *A Theology of the New Testament* (Grand Rapids: Eerdmans, 1974), 339.

3. Stephen G. Hatfield, "The Lordship of Christ: A Biblical Analysis," *Southwestern Journal of Theology* 33 (Spring 1991, No. 2), 16.

4. "Letter of a Recruit: Apion," in Select Papyri I (1932) #112 (II.A.D.), cited in Hatfield, "The Lordship of Christ," 16. See www.csun.edu/~hcfll004/paplet1.htm, accessed 8/24/2006.

5. "Text of the Rosetta Stone," at www.thebritishmuseum.ac.uk, accessed 8/24/2006. The stone was bilingual, being inscribed in both Egyptian scripts and Greek. The text celebrated the reign of Ptolemy in his ninth year, 196 B.C. For a discussion of the use of *kurios*, see Hatfield, "The Lordship of Christ," 16–25. For a list of examples of *kurios* in secular sources, see Walter Bauer, *A Greek-English Lexicon of the New Testament and Other Early Christian Literature* (Chicago: The University of Chicago Press, 1979), 458–461; and Gerhard Kittel, *Theological Dictionary of the New Testament*, vol. III (Grand Rapids: Eerdmans, 1965), 1039–1098.

6. Gerhard Kittel, *Theological Dictionary, III*, 1056.

7. See Walter Bauer, *A Greek-English Lexicon*, 459.

8. This story is based on accounts found in historical documents. See Henry Bettenson, "The Martyrdom of Polycarp," from *Martyrium Polycarpi* [A letter from the Church of Smyrna], *Documents of the Early Christian Church*, (New York: Oxford Press, 1963), 9-12.

9. Gerhard Kittel, *Theological Dictionary*, III, 1048-1049.

10. Gerhard Kittel, *Theological Dictionary*, III, 1049, note 25.

11. See Stephen G. Hatfield, "The Lordship of Christ," 17. God designates himself as "Yahweh" in Exod. 3.

12. Gerhard Kittel, *Theological Dictionary*, III, 1061.

13. Stephen G. Hatfield, "The Lordship of Christ," 17.

14. See parallels in Matt. 22:41-46 and Luke 20:41-44.

15. See Donald Guthrie, *New Testament Theology* (Downers Grove: InterVarsity Press, 1981), 293. Also see John 13:13, where Jesus said, "You call Me Teacher and Lord; and right are you, for so I am."

16. F.F. Bruce, *Jesus, Lord and Savior* (Downers Grove: InterVarsity Press, 1986), 200.

17. Stephen G. Hatfield, "The Lordship of Christ", 19. See also Jerome H. Negrey, "My Lord and My God: The Divinity of Jesus in John's Gospel," in SBL 1986 Seminar Papers, ed. Kent H. Richards (Atlanta: Scholars Press, 1986), 152-171.

18. Stephen G. Hatfield, "The Lordship of Christ," 19.

19. Luke is commonly believed to be the author of Acts.

20. Stephen G. Hatfield, "The Lordship of Christ," 19.

21. See also Peter's sermon to Cornelius's household, Acts 10:34-43, where he proclaimed in 10:36, "The word which He sent to the sons of Israel, preaching peace through Jesus Christ (He is Lord of all)." Employing the idea of Lordship with a Gentile audience, Peter asserted that Jesus' Lordship extends over all people everywhere. No ethnic boundaries can be applied to his Lordship.

22. Stephen G. Hatfield, "The Lordship of Christ," 19.

23. Luke's writings contain 210 references to *kurios*.

24. William L. Lumpkin, "Lordship of Christ," www.mercer.edu/baptiststudies/CTest/HC/lord.htm, accessed 8/24/2006.

25. "Somerset Baptist Confession," as found in William L. Lumpkin, *Baptist Confessions of Faith* (Philadelphia: Judson Press, 1969), 208.

26. "The Faith and Practice of Thirty Congregations," 1651, in Lumpkin, *Baptist Confessions of Faith*, 178, italics in original.

27. William L. Lumpkin, "Lordship of Christ," 2.

Chapter Two

1. Marcus J. Borg and N. T. Wright, *The Meaning of Jesus: Two Visions* (San Francisco: Harper Collins, 2000), 157.

2. In 1 Cor. 5:9, Paul states, "I wrote to you in my letter not to associate with immoral people." This may imply that Paul had written a previous letter which is now lost. 1 Corinthians, therefore, may be the second letter Paul wrote to the church in Corinth.

3. Thomas Cahill, *Desire of the Everlasting Hills: The World Before and After Jesus* (New York: Doubleday, 1999), 257.

4. Marcus J. Borg, *Meeting Jesus Again for the First Time* (New York: Harper Collins, 1995), 29. For a good summary of the quest for the historical Jesus, see N.T. Wright, *Who Was Jesus?* (Grand Rapids: Eerdmans, 1992), 1–18.

5. Borg and Wright, *The Meaning of Jesus*, 146.

6. Philip Yancey, *The Jesus I Never Knew* (Grand Rapids: Zondervan, 1995), 19.

7. See Millard J. Erickson, *Christian Theology,* 2nd ed. (Grand Rapids: Baker Academic, 2005), 702.

8. Matt.1:20; 11:25; Acts 17:24; Rev. 4:11.

9. Luke 2:11; John 20:28; Acts 10:36; 1 Cor. 2:8; Phil. 2:11; James 2:1; Rev. 19:16.

10. Erickson, *Christian Theology*, 708.

11. See Acts 2:20–21, from Joel 2:31–32; Rom. 10:13, from Joel 2:32; 1 Pet. 3:15, from Isa. 8:13.

12. F. F. Bruce, *Jesus: Lord and Savior,* (Downers Grove, IL: InterVarsity Press, 1986), 204.

13. George Eldon Ladd, *A Theology of the New Testament* (Grand Rapids: Eerdmans, 1974), 165.

14. See also Mark 3:11.

15. Ladd, *A Theology of the New Testament*, 165.

16. Rom. 1:4; 2 Cor. 1:19; Gal. 2:20; Eph. 4:13.

17. Heb. 4:14; 6:6; 7:3; 10:29.

18. 1 John 3:8; 4:15; 5:5, 10, 12, 13, 20; Rev. 2:18.

19. Ladd, *A Theology of the New Testament*, 165.

20. Compare Luke 10:21–22. See Ladd, *A Theology of the New Testament*, 166.

21. See Matt. 5:21–22, 27–28, 31–32, 33–34, 38–39, 43–44.

22. Jacob Neusner, *A Rabbi Talks With Jesus* (New York: Doubleday, 1993), 24, 29, 31, 53, cited in Yancey, *The Jesus I Never Knew*, 96.

23. N.T. Wright in Borg and Wright, *The Meaning of Jesus*, 44.

24. N.T. Wright in Borg and Wright, *The Meaning of Jesus*, 46.

25. N.T. Wright, *The Original Jesus* (Grand Rapids: Eerdmans, 1996), 61–62.

26. Wright, *The Original Jesus,* 62.

27. See N. T. Wright, *The Challenge of Jesus* (Downers Grove, Illinois: InterVarsity Press, 1999), 110–111. Note Matt. 27:51. The temple veil was torn asunder—top to bottom—as Jesus surrendered his life on the cross.

28. N. T. Wright, *The Challenge of Jesus,* 114.

29. For an extended study see N. T Wright, *Jesus and the Victory of God* (Minneapolis: Fortress Press, 1996), 432–437.

30. The term *synoptic* is used to describe the three Gospels that are most alike. *Synoptic* means *with the same eye*. These Gospels are called *synoptic* because they seem to see Jesus in similar ways. John presents a unique, although not contradictory, portrait of Jesus.

31. For other examples of "I am" sayings in John with divine implications see 6:35 (bread of life); 8:12 and 9:5 (the light of the world); 8:23 (from above); 8:24 (you will die in your sins unless you believe I am He); 8:28 (I am He); 10:11 (the good shepherd); 11:25 (the resurrection and the life); 14:6 (the way, and the truth, and the life); 15:1 (the true vine); 18:5 (I am He).

32. N.T. Wright, *The Challenge of Jesus*, 106.

33. Tom (N.T.) Wright, *John for Everyone, Part 1*, (Cambridge: University Press, 2002), 157.

34. See Roger E. Olsen, *The Story of Christian Theology: Twenty Centuries of Tradition and Reform* (Downers Grove, Illinois: InterVarsity Press, 1999), 137 and following.

35. C. S. Lewis, *Mere Christianity* (New York: Simon and Schuster, 1980), 56.

Chapter Three

1. See Isaiah 2:12; 10:3; 13:6, 9; 34:8; Ezekiel 7:19; 13:5; 30:3; Joel 1:15; 2:11; Amos 5:18; Zephaniah 1:14; Zechariah 14:1.

2. G. R. Beasley-Murray, *Jesus and the Kingdom of God* (Grand Rapids: Eerdmans, 1986), 11–12. See also Joel 2.

3. G. R. Beasley-Murray, *Jesus and the Kingdom of God*, 15.

4. G. R. Beasley-Murray, *Jesus and the Kingdom of God*, 17.

5. See also Exodus 15:18; Numbers 23:21; 2 Kings 19:15; Psalm 99:1–4; Isaiah 43:15; Jeremiah 46:18.

6. The concept of the kingship of God can be linked back to the enthronement psalms (Psalms 47; 93; 96–99). In these psalms, we find a hymn-like confession that Yahweh has become King and the Lord reigns. See Leonhard Goppelt, *A Theology of the New Testament, Vol. 1, The Ministry of Jesus and Its Theological Significance* (Grand Rapids: Eerdmans, 1981), 45–46.

7. Isa. 26:1–15; 28:5–6; Ezek. 11:17–20; Hosea 2:6–17; Zech. 8:1–8.

8. Isa. 49:22–26; 60:4–16; Amos 9:11–12; Micah 4:13; 7:8–17.

9. Isa. 25:6–7; 45:21–22; 51:4–5; 52:10–11; 56:3–7; Jer. 3:17; Zeph. 3:8–9; Zech. 8:20–21; 14:9. G. R. Beasley-Murray, *Jesus and the Kingdom of God*, 20.

10. Isa. 1:25–26; 4:3–4; 32:15–16; 52:13—53:12; Jer. 31:31–34; Ezek. 36:25–26; 37:23–24.

11. Isa. 35; 41:17–18; Ezek. 47; Hosea 2:21–22; Joel 3:18; Amos 9:13.

12. Isa. 12; 33:17–24; Jer. 31:1–14; Hosea 2:14–15; 14:4–5; Zeph. 3:14–20.

13. Because the immediate audience of the Gospel of Matthew likely had a Jewish background and because of Matthew's respect for the divine name, Matthew most often describes the kingdom as the "kingdom of heaven."

14. N. T. Wright, *The Challenge of Jesus* (Downers Grove, IL: InterVarsity Press, 1999), 37.

15. N.T. Wright, *The Challenge of Jesus*, 37, and Donald Guthrie, *New Testament Theology* (Downers Grove: InterVarsity Press, 1981), 411.

16. George Eldon Ladd, *A Theology of the New Testament* (Grand Rapids: Eerdmans, 1974), 57.

17. N. T. Wright, *The Challenge of Jesus*, 46.

18. Robert Stein, *Luke*, New American Commentary (Nashville: Broadman Press, 1992), 157–159.

19. Matt. 12:32; Mark 10:30; Luke 16:8; 20:34–36; Rom. 12:2; 1 Cor. 2:6, 8; 10:11; 2 Cor. 4:4; Gal. 1:4; 1 Tim. 6:17; 2 Tim. 4:10; Titus 2:12; Heb. 6:5; 2 Peter 3:13.

20. Thus, the present age extends from creation until the day of the Lord.

21. Because the kingdom came in unexpected ways, accomplished by an unexpected person, Jesus, the Jews did not recognize its arrival.

22. George Eldon Ladd, *A Theology of the New Testament*, 48.

23. See also Acts 20:24–25.

24. Donald Guthrie, *New Testament Theology*, 429.

Chapter Four

1. For an attempt to come to some factual conclusions about the resurrection appearances, see Leonard Goppelt, *A Theology of the New Testament,* vol. 1 (Grand Rapids: Eerdmans, 1981), 239–240.

2. George Eldon Ladd, *A Theology of the New Testament* (Grand Rapids: Eerdmans, 1974), 315.

3. N. T. Wright, *The Resurrection of the Son of God* (Minneapolis: Fortress Press, 2003), 568.

4. Paul Smith, *Jesus: Meet Him Again for the First Time* (Gresham, Oregon: Vision House Publishing, Inc., 1994), 149.

5. Paul Smith, *Jesus*, 151.

6. Philip Yancey, *The Jesus I Never Knew* (Grand Rapids: Zondervan, 1995), 212.

7. Except John the Apostle (John 19:26).

8. Now actually eleven, with Judas not yet replaced.

9. Note, though, that the resurrected Jesus expounded from Scripture to show how he should suffer and yet rise again on the third day (Luke 24:45–46).

10. George Eldon Ladd, *A Theology of the New Testament*, 316.

11. N. T. Wright, *The Challenge of Jesus* (Downers Grove, Illinois: InterVarsity Press, 1999), 139.

12. N.T. Wright, *The Resurrection of the Son of God*, 570.

13. Calvin Miller, *The Book of Jesus* (New York: Simon and Schuster, 1996), 463.

14. George Eldon Ladd, *A Theology of the New Testament*, 317.

15. N.T. Wright, *The Challenge of Jesus*, 126.

16. Donald Guthrie, *New Testament Theology* (Downers Grove, Illinois: InterVarsity Press, 1981), 375.

17. Floyd V. Filson, *Jesus Christ, The Risen Lord* (New York/Nashville: Abingdon, 1956), 48.

18. George Eldon Ladd, *A Theology of the New Testament*, 317. Marcus Borg wrote that God's resurrection of Jesus from the dead was "the foundational affirmation of the New Testament." See Marcus Borg and N. T. Wright, *The Meaning of Jesus: Two Visions*, (San Francisco: HarperCollins, 2000), 129.

19. A recent work by New Testament scholar James Tabor of the University of North Carolina at Charlotte contradicts my position. Tabor concluded that Jesus tried to set up an earthly kingdom but failed at his task. Tabor rejects the resurrection of Jesus. Tabor says that Jesus' movement survived by re-centering on a new leader, James, the brother of Jesus. See James D. Tabor, *The Jesus Dynasty: The Hidden History of Jesus, His Royal Family, and the Birth of Christianity* (New York: Simon and Schuster, 2006), 228, 234, 240, 244.

20. Marcus Borg and N. T. Wright, *The Meaning of Jesus*, 111.

21. N.T. Wright, *The Challenge of Jesus*, 126.

22. See F. F. Bruce, *Jesus: Lord and Savior* (Downers Grove, IL: InterVarsity Press, 1986), 118.

23. Leonhard Goppelt believed that the language of the formula is not Pauline and that it came from early Greek-speaking Jewish Christianity that perhaps even went back to an Aramaic prototype. Leonhard Goppelt, *A Theology of the New Testament*, 233.

24. For other passages outside of Paul's letters that emphasize the resurrection, see these references in Luke and Acts: Luke 24:7, 34; Acts 3:15; 4:2, 10, 33; 5:30; 10:39–41; 13:37; 17:31; 25:19.

25. Donald Guthrie, *New Testament Theology*, 296.

26. Donald Guthrie, *New Testament Theology*, 292; George Eldon Ladd, *A Theology of the New Testament*, 338.

27. Donald Guthrie, *New Testament Theology*, 292–293.

28. Marcus Borg and N. T. Wright, *The Meaning of Jesus,* 129.

29. Marcus Borg and N. T. Wright, *The Meaning of Jesus*, 136.

30. Floyd Filson, *Jesus Christ, The Risen Lord*, 51.

31. See Marcus Borg and N. T. Wright, *The Meaning of Jesus*, 136. For texts that deal with Christ's exaltation see John 20:17; Phil. 2:6–11; and 1 Pet. 3:22.

32. N. T. Wright, *The Challenge of Jesus*, 135.

33. Marcus Borg and N. T. Wright, *The Meaning of Jesus*, 112.

34. Marcus Borg and N. T. Wright, *The Meaning of Jesus*, 115.

35. Several people in the New Testament (including Lazarus, Jairus's daughter, and the son of the widow of Nain) were brought back to life, but their "resuscitation" from death did not begin the age of the resurrection for God's people. They had to face death again at a later date. See F. F. Bruce, *Jesus, Lord and Savior*, 122.
36. George Eldon Ladd, *A Theology of the New Testament*, 326.
37. N. T. Wright, *The Challenge of Jesus*, 132.
38. George Eldon Ladd, *A Theology of the New Testament*, 318.
39. N. T. Wright, *The Challenge of Jesus*, 138.
40. N. T. Wright, *The Challenge of Jesus*, 140.
41. N. T. Wright, *The Original Jesus*, 75.
42. Calvin Miller, *The Book of Jesus*, 458.
43. N. T. Wright, *Resurrection of the Son of God*, 579.

Chapter Five

1. "Spirituality May Be Hot in America, But 76 Million Adults Never Attend Church," *Barna Update*, March 20, 2006. See www.barna.org. Accessed 8/24/2006.
2. "Americans Have Commitment Issues," *Barna Update*, April 18, 2006. See www.barna.org. Accessed 8/24/2006.
3. Rodney Clapp, *A Peculiar People* (Downers Grove, IL: InterVarsity Press, 1996), 89.
4. See Rom. 2:28–29; 4:11–18; 9:7–8; Gal. 3:29.
5. Philip Yancey, *Church: Why Bother?* (Grand Rapids, Michigan: Zondervan, 1998), 64. See also Stanley Hauerwas and William H. Willimon, *Resident Aliens* (Nashville: Abingdon Press, 1989), 154.
6. Rodney Clapp, *A Peculiar People*, 100.
7. This imagery appears in many places in the New Testament. Here are but a few: Matthew 5:23; 18:15, 35; Acts 9:17; Rom. 14:21; 1 Cor. 1:1; 7:12; 2 Cor. 1:1; Phil. 2:25; Col. 4:9; James 2:15; Rev. 1:9. For specific references to sisters, see Rom. 16:1; 1 Cor. 7:15; James 2:15; 2 John 13.
8. Robert Sloan, "Images of the Church in Paul," Paul Basden and David Dockery, *The People of God: Essays on the Believers' Church* (Nashville: Baptist Sunday School Board, 1991), 150.
9. *Ekklesia* is also sometimes used to describe the church universal, all believers throughout the ages. See Eph. 1:22; 3:10; 5:22–27; Col. 1:24.
10. *Ekklesia* is used only three times in the Gospels (Matt. 16:18; 18:17) and more than sixty times in the traditional letters of Paul.
11. Robert Sloan, "The People of God," 153.
12. G. W. Bromley, "Church," *The International Standard Bible Encyclopedia*, Vol. 1 (Grand Rapids: Eerdmans, 1979), 693.

13. Donald Guthrie, *New Testament Theology* (Downers Grove, IL: InterVarsity Press, 1981), 703. Parables about the kingdom, moreover, sometimes carry the idea of a growing community (Mark 4:30-32).

14. Howard Batson, *Common-Sense Church Growth* (Macon, GA: Smyth & Helwys, 1999), 115.

15. Philip Yancey, *Church: Why Bother*, 26.

16. Dietrich Bonhoeffer, *The Cost of Discipleship* (New York: MacMillan, 1963), 45-47.

17. Darrell L. Guder, *Missional Church: A Vision for the Sending of the Church in North America* (Grand Rapids: Eerdmans, 1998), 83-84.

18. Philip Yancey, *Church: Why Bother*, 78.

19. Rodney Clapp, *A Peculiar People*, 197.

20. Fred B. Craddock, *Craddock Stories*, (St. Louis, MO: Chalice Press, 2001), 46.

21. Fred B. Craddock, *Craddock Stories*, 132.

22. Thornton Wilder, *Our Town: A Play in Three Acts* (New York: Harper & Row, Publishers, 1938), 81, italics in original.

23. Adapted from William Shakespeare, *Hamlet*, Act 5, Scene 2.

24. Fred B. Craddock, *Craddock Stories*, 14.

Chapter Six

1. See Ronald J. Sider, *The Scandal of the Evangelical Conscience* (Grand Rapids: Baker Books, 2005), 13.

2. See Jim Wallis, *The Call to Conversion: Recovering the Gospel for These Times* (San Francisco: Harper Collins, 1992), 20.

3. Ronald J. Sider, *The Scandal of the Evangelical Conscience*, 13. See, for example, the various reports at www.barna.org. Accessed 8/25/2006.

4. See Tim Stafford, "The Third Coming of George Barna," *Christianity Today* (August 5, 2002), www.ctlibrary.com/8673. Accessed 8/25/2006.

5. Gary C. Redding, *Preaching* (March/April 2000), 16.

6. C. S. Lewis, *The Screwtape Letters* (New York: Mentor, A Division of Penguin Books USA, 1988), 117.

7. John DeGraaf, David Wann, and Thomas N. Naylor, *Affluenza* (San Francisco: Berrett-Koehler Publishers, Inc., 2001), 2.

8. John DeGraaf, *Affluenza*, 3.

9. John DeGraaf, *Affluenza*, 13.

10. Mark Buchanan, "Trapped in the Cult of the Next Thing," *Christianity Today* (September 6, 1999), 63-71.

11. "The Diderot Effect," *Homiletics* (August 1999), 62.

12. Robert H. Frank, *Luxury Fever: Money and Happiness in an Era of Excess* (Princeton, NJ: Princeton University Press, 1999), 6.

13. "The Rich, The Poor, and the Growing Gap Between Them," *The Economist* (June 17, 2006), 28-30. See also "Inequality and the American Dream," *The Economist* (June 17, 2006), 13-14.

14. Ronald J. Sider, *The Scandal of the Evangelical Conscience*, 20.
15. See www.emptytomb.org/research.html#Fig1. Accessed 8/25/2006.
16. "Pass the Offering Plate," *The Christian Century* (September 7, 2004). See also www.emptytomb.org/scg036Potential.php. Accessed 8/25/2006.
17. See www.emptytomb.org/potential.html. Accessed 8/25/2006. See also Carol Bellamy, "The State of The World's Children 2001," www.unicef.org/sowc01/short_version/page3.htm. Accessed 8/25/2006.
18. Jim Wallis, *The Call to Conversion*, 18.
19. Michael J. Silverstein, *Treasure Hunt: Inside the Mind of the New Consumer* (New York: The Penguin Group, 2006), 6. Market analyst Michael J. Silverstein presents the Boston Consulting Group's "Average Upper-Middle-Market Income Statement." The report shows the average upper-middle income family as having $100,000 of annual pretax income with charitable gifts of only $2,400 (2.4%). This independent study by the Boston Consulting Group confirmed the results of previous studies on charitable giving.
20. Ronald J. Sider, *The Scandal of the Evangelical Conscience*, 22.
21. Barbara Dafoe Whitehead, *The Divorce Culture* (New York: Vintage Books, 1996), 11.
22. The Barna Group. "Born Again Christians Just As Likely to Divorce As Are Non-Christians," March 8, 2004. See www.barna.org/FlexPage.aspx?Page=BarnaUpdate&BarnaUpdateID=170. Accessed 8/25/2006.
23. Blaine Harden, "Bible Belt Couples 'Put Asunder' More, Despite New Efforts," *New York Times*, May 21, 2001, A-14.
24. The Barna Group, "Born Again Adults Less Likely to Co-Habit, Just As Likely to Divorce," August 6, 2001. See www.barna.org/FlexPage.aspx?Page=BarnaUpdate&BarnaUpdateID=95. Accessed 8/25/2006.
25. For examples, see Alan Cooperman, "Case of Gay Worshiper in Va. Splits Methodists," *Washington Post*, October 28, 2005, A11; Associated Press with Don Munsch, "Presbyterians to Address Homosexuality," *Amarillo Globe-News*, June 23, 2000, www.amarillo.com/stories/062300/new_149-3338.shtml ; Richard N. Ostling, "Clergy Split Over Gay Marriage," *Lexington Herald-Leader*, June 4, 2006, A3; "Lutheran Task Force: Bible Supports Homosexual Unions," *The Greenville News*, October 20, 1993, 4A; and Hilary Appelman, "Presbyterians Deny Pastorate to Lesbian," *Waco Tribune Herald*, November 5, 1992, 3A.
26. For a more extensive history of the treatment of homosexuality by the mental health community, see Howard K. Batson, *The Relevance of Romans 1 for the Nature/Nurture Debate Regarding Homosexuality* (Ann Arbor, MI: UMI, 1995), 157ff.
27. Charles C. Mann, "Behavioral Genetics in Transition," *Science* 264 (June 17, 1994), 1687.
28. Martin Luther King, Jr. "Remaining Awake Through a Great Revolution." Delivered at the National Cathedral, Washington, D.C., on March 31, 1968. See www.africanamericans.com/MLKRemainingAwakeThroughGreatRevolution.htm. Accessed 8/25/2006.

29. The church I serve as pastor, First Baptist Church of Amarillo, Texas, supports several "focused" congregations.

30. Cited in Marv Knox, "Segregation Undermines Churches' Ability to Reach Society With Gospel," published January 24, 2006. See www.abpnews.com/788.article. Accessed 8/25/2006.

31. C. Peter Wagner, "The Fourth Dimension of Missions: Strategy," *Perspectives on the World Christian Movement* (Pasadena, CA: William Carey Library, 1981), 579.

32. C. Peter Wagner, "The Fourth Dimension," 579.

33. Clarence Jordan, *A Substance of Faith: And Other Cotton Patch Sermons* (Eugene, OR: Wipf and Stock Publishers, 2005), 115.

34. John W. Kennedy, "Big Dream in Little Rock," *Christianity Today* (April 2005), 42–43.

35. Eugene C. Roehlkepartain, "From Age Segregation to Intergenerational Community," *The Clergy Journal* (October 2003), 7–9.

Chapter Seven

1. See Ernst Haenchen, *The Acts of the Apostles* (Philadelphia: The Westminster Press, 1971), 180–183.

2. See William J. Larkin, Jr., *Acts*, The IVP New Testament Commentary Series (Downers Grove, IL: InterVarsity Press, 1995), 50–51.

3. See John B. Polhill, *Acts*, The New American Commentary (Nashville: Broadman Press, 1992), 254–256.

4. See Donald Guthrie, *New Testament Theology* (Downers Grove, IL: InterVarsity Press, 1981), 294.

5. See Frances W. Beare, *The Gospel According to Matthew* (Peabody, MA: Hendrickson Publishers, 1981), 198.

6. See also Matt. 16:27; 25:31–46; John 5:22, 27, 29; 1 Cor. 4:5; 11:32; 2 Cor. 5:10; and 2 Tim. 4:1, 8.

7. See F. F. Bruce, *Jesus: Lord and Savior* (Downers Grove, IL: InterVarsity Press, 1986), 191; see also N.T. Wright, *The Challenge of Jesus* (Downers Grove, IL: InterVarsity Press, 1999), 180.

8. George Eldon Ladd, *A Theology of the New Testament* (Grand Rapids, MI: Eerdmans, 1974), 158.

9. George Eldon Ladd, *A Theology of the New Testament*, 630.

10. Baptists, unfortunately, sometimes emphasize Christ's crucifixion and resurrection to the exclusion of his ascension and enthronement.

11. Marcus J. Borg and N. T. Wright, *The Meaning of Jesus: Two Visions* (New York: HarperSanFrancisco, 1999), 201.

12. Donald Guthrie, *New Testament Theology*, 295.

13. Donald Guthrie, *New Testament Theology*, 295–296.

14. F. F. Bruce, *Jesus: Lord and Savior*, 188.

15. Robert H. Stein, *Luke*, The New American Commentary (Nashville: Broadman Press, 1992), 147.

16. George Eldon Ladd, *A Theology of the New Testament*, 50.

17. George Eldon Ladd, *A Theology of the New Testament*, 68.

18. On another occasion, Satan wanted to lay his hands on Peter to prove the weakness of Peter's faith (Luke 22:31-32). Peter was saved by the prayer of Christ.

19. See these accounts of Jesus exorcising demons: Matt. 9:32-34; Mark 1:23; 5:1-20; 7:24-30; 9:14-29; Luke 8:26-39.

20. See A. J. Bandstra, "Principalities and Powers," *The New International Standard Bible Encyclopedia 3* (Grand Rapids, MI: Eerdmans, 1988), 971.

21. For an extensive discussion on principalities and powers, see Walter Wink, *Naming The Powers* (Philadelphia: Fortress Press, 1984), 151-163.

22. A. J. Bandstra, "Principalities and Powers," *The New International Standard Bible Encyclopedia 3*, 972.

23. See John Howard Yoder, *The Politics of Jesus* (Grand Rapids, MI: Eerdmans, 1972), 147-161.

24. N. T. Wright, *The Challenge of Jesus* (Downers Grove, Illinois: InterVarsity Press, 1999), 114.

25. See George Eldon Ladd, *A Theology of the New Testament*, 630.

Conclusion

1. See chapter 3, note 1.

2. N. T. Wright, *The Challenge of Jesus* (Downers Grove, IL: InterVarsity Press, 1999), 126.

3. Donald Guthrie, *New Testament Theology* (Downers Grove, IL: InterVarsity Press, 1981), 375.

4. Donald Guthrie, *New Testament Theology*, 296.

5. See chapter 5, note 7.

How to Order More Study Materials

It's easy! Just fill in the following information. For additional Bible study materials, see www.baptistwaypress.org or get a complete order form of available materials by calling 1–866–249–1799 or e-mailing baptistway@bgct.org.

Title of item	Price	Quantity	Cost
This Issue:			
Jesus Is Lord!	$5.95	_____	_____
Jesus Is Lord!—Teaching Guide	$1.95	_____	_____
Additional Baptist Doctrine and Heritage studies			
The Bible—You Can Believe It	$4.95	_____	_____
The Bible—You Can Believe It—Teaching Guide	$1.95	_____	_____
Beliefs Important to Baptists			
Beliefs Important to Baptists—Study Guide (one-volume edition; includes all lessons)	$2.35	_____	_____
Beliefs Important to Baptists—Teaching Guide (one-volume edition; includes all lessons)	$1.95	_____	_____
Who in the World Are Baptists, Anyway? (one lesson)	$ .45	_____	_____
Who in the World Are Baptists, Anyway?—Teacher's Edition	$ .55	_____	_____
Beliefs Important to Baptists: I (four lessons)	$1.35	_____	_____
Beliefs Important to Baptists: I—Teacher's Edition	$1.75	_____	_____
Beliefs Important to Baptists: II (four lessons)	$1.35	_____	_____
Beliefs Important to Baptists: II—Teacher's Edition	$1.75	_____	_____
Beliefs Important to Baptists: III (four lessons)	$1.35	_____	_____
Beliefs Important to Baptists: III—Teacher's Edition	$1.75	_____	_____
For Children			
Let's Explore Baptist Beliefs	$3.95	_____	_____
Let's Explore Baptist Beliefs—Leader's Guide	$2.95	_____	_____

Cost of items (Order value) _____
Processing fee (1% of Cost of Items) _____
Shipping charges (see chart*) _____
TOTAL _____

Standard (UPS/Mail) Shipping Charges*	
Order Value	Shipping charge
$.01–$9.99	$5.00
$10.00–$19.99	$6.00
$20.00–$39.99	$7.00
$40.00–$79.99	$8.00
$80.00–$99.99	$11.00
$100.00–$129.99	$13.00
$130.00–$149.99	$17.00
$150.00–$199.99	$20.00
$200.00–$299.99	$25.00
$300.00 and up	10% of order value

*Plus, applicable taxes for individuals and other taxable entities (not churches) within Texas will be added. Please call 1–866–249–1799 if the exact amount is needed prior to ordering.

Please allow three weeks for standard delivery. For express shipping service: Call 1–866–249–1799 for information on additional charges.

YOUR NAME   PHONE

_____

YOUR CHURCH   DATE ORDERED

_____

MAILING ADDRESS

_____

CITY   STATE   ZIP CODE

MAIL this form with your check for the total amount to:

BAPTISTWAY PRESS
Baptist General Convention of Texas
333 North Washington
Dallas, TX 75246-1798

(Make checks to "Baptist Executive Board.")

OR, **FAX** your order anytime to: 214-828-5376, and we will bill you.

OR, **CALL** your order toll-free: 1-866-249-1799
(M-Th 8:30 a.m.–8:30 p.m.; Fri 8:30 a.m.–5:00 p.m.), and we will bill you.

OR, **E-MAIL** your order to our internet e-mail address:
baptistway@bgct.org, and we will bill you.

OR, ORDER **ONLINE** at www.baptistwaypress.org.

We look forward to receiving your order! Thank you!